WOMEN OF POWER AND UTILITIES

Connie Turner Carden

iucx
INNOVATE UTILITYCX | Aspiring Authors
an iucx publication

Sherman, TX

Disclaimer: The recommendations, advice, descriptions and methods in this book are presented solely for educational purposes. The author and publisher assume no liability whatsoever for any loss or damage that results from the use of any of the material in this book. Use of the material in this book is solely at the risk of the user.

Printed in the United States of America
Hardcover ISBN: 978-0-9961360-6-8
Ebook ISBN: 978-0-9961360-7-5

IUCX Aspiring Authors
2612 W Lamberth Rd, Ste 300
Sherman, TX 75092
www.iucx.org
903-893-3214

Dedicated to my beloved parents, Sarah and Robert Turner, whose unwavering belief in me made the impossible seem within reach, and to my dear husband Clint, whose support made the impossible reality.

TABLE OF CONTENTS

FOREWORD

I met Connie Carden more than a decade ago while masking my nerves as I waited for a conference hall to be invaded by swarms of industry professionals about to witness my public-speaking catastrophe.

Having never spoken publicly to so large an audience, the only thing I confidently knew was that in just under an hour, my presentation would be a career-shattering embarrassment. While mapping out the quickest exit (the heck with a graceful retreat!), Connie approached me and introduced herself.

Thoughts of "Who is this chick and why is she talking to me?" and "Doesn't this lady know I am busy freaking out and trying to pray?" swirled in my head. I prepared to respond with, "Look, lady, you can catch me after the circus… if you still want to!" Unbeknownst to me, it was because Connie had seen through my masked nerves that she was extending more than just a hand of introduction. She had extended her hand to pull me out of my mental quagmire.

Not only had Connie seen through my flawed attempt to appear as though I had everything under control, but she also saw *me* – a young, professional woman of color trying to understand how to best navigate a space that felt too big for me, a space which transcended that conference hall. Today, I am convinced that Connie showed up in response to my frantic, inaudible prayer.

"Do you know what I find helpful when speaking at venues like this?", she asked. "I like to greet people as they come in," she coached, "ask them for their name and what they are looking to learn. Then, I refer to them and their interests while I am speaking. This makes it personal and more conversational, allowing you to just be yourself. Relax and have fun with this," she continued. "I will be in the front row cheering you on." Indeed, Connie did sit in the front row with an encouraging smile that never faltered during my 45-minute oration.

All these years later, those sensible tips she gave me that hot morning in North Carolina have continued to be as impactful as the treasured memory of her *showing up* and caring. I survived that speaking engagement and have *maneuvered* dozens more since, as a business process automation, analytics and artificial intelligence (AI) leader.

While I was tempted to use generative AI to assist with writing this Foreword (I am kidding, Connie!), so much of what we encounter in life is already artificial. Consider how rare it is to encounter something real. From grass to sweeteners, we are accustomed to substitutes.

There is nothing artificial here. For those who have met or will meet Connie, she is as unforgettable as her distinguished Southern dialect. Unfiltered, uncomfortably direct and humorously raw, she is as real as this book's genuine acknowledgement of women who continue to help others personally and professionally.

In our world where we define progress by the visible and tangible, the impacts of leadership flow from the consistent currents of influence that transform perspectives and redefine industries. Each chapter represents a *real* testament to the relatable journey of a woman who has defied barriers while dedicating their careers and personal lives to equipping others to do the same.

It is not only okay to need others but also normal. In fact, we allow ourselves to grow as we nurture growth in others, connect with them and relate to them. We are, after all, social creatures and not isolated islands – metaphorically speaking, that is. As you read about each of the women Connie pays tribute to in this book, you will find their stories surprisingly relatable.

I encountered one such surprise as I read Connie's own chapter in this book. Her own dislike for public speaking rivaled my own. Ha! Little did I know that those many years ago when she connected a part of herself with me in that brief encouraging interaction, she was encouraging herself.

Simple interactions can have surprising impacts. Imagine what we could accomplish if more of us followed her example by amplifying and magnifying what is common instead of what is different.

Let us not underestimate the power of a kind word or compassionate smile as we look beyond ourselves to see those who think they are invisible and empower them to shine.

In a world where there isn't a shortage of words, opinions, posts and stories, it's easy to sound trite, glib and insipid. And yet, as we live, look and listen with intentionality like the women you will read about here, our lives too will soar when we help shape, serve, succor and strengthen others. How? Through storytelling.

Each of us has a story. Each of us is a story. Much like the pages in this book, the pages of our lives are written with the inks of joys, griefs, triumphs, trials, successes, failures. There is a thread that binds us inconspicuously to another's story. The unique ways we use our *superpowers* and their potential to impact others can only be realized if we share the stories we have – the stories that we are.

The influences of each woman profiled, and the author herself, extend far beyond the walls of any single organization. In fields traditionally dominated by men, each of these women has used her *superpowers* to create opportunities for others, opening doors that were once closed and paving the way for a more inclusive and diverse industry. Their disparate approaches are holistic, recognizing that lasting impact comes from supporting both the personal and professional growth of others.

In reading their stories, we have an opportunity to challenge ourselves with a call to action, to lift others as we climb, to hold up those beside us in our journeys, to push others beyond the boundaries of our own perceived limitations or shortcomings, and to leave a legacy of empowerment that transcends spaces, physical and metaphysical, and generations.

Rockie Solomon

INTRODUCTION

Why did I write this book? Believe me, I asked myself that question every week since its inception in June 2023. However, I did not think up this journey by myself. It was the brainchild of Eversource's Executive Vice President Penni McLean Conner, the author of three books, *Customer Service: Utility Style*, *Energy Efficiency: Principles and Practices*, and *Profiles in Excellence: Utility Chief Customer Officers*.

One evening at CS Week in May of 2023, Penni suggested that I author a book. I replied, "Penni, I am too busy with my job and my family, traveling and trying to have a life. The last thing I need is something else that demands time."

And besides all that, I am no writer. English is my second language behind Southern, and anyone trying to decipher my emails would be the first to agree.

After a big throaty laugh (for which she is famous), Penni asked again. She can be very stubborn once she decides you need to do something, so 'resistance is futile.'

I remembered her *Profiles in Excellence* book where she interviewed nine trailblazers in the utility industry that served as chief customer officers and told their stories of success.

Then, it came to me. "Penni, what if I profiled women like me who serve the utility industry in a consulting or vendor capacity and how they managed their way to the top of their field? Would that work? Women from companies like IBM, SAP, Accenture, KPMG, Oracle and the like?" She replied, "If you can name five women immediately, you have your book."

I named nine, and so this book was born.

Many books have been written about great leaders who work for the utility as an employee, but few have been written about the women (and men) who serve those professionals. When I first started working at Price Waterhouse in the 1980s, there were few women sitting in meetings with me helping our utility clients solve business problems. But today, consulting and sales partners have learned that women in sales and delivery roles help build relationships that last years, and clients always buy from people whom they like.

This book is a tribute to nine women whom I have either worked with directly, watched from afar or directly competed against over my 40-plus year career. Their stories span decades, from Patty Bruffy who began her career in the '70s to Laura Sciuto who is just getting started.

When I asked each of these women if they wanted to be profiled, their response was either one of shock or one of tears. 'Why would you want to write about me? I am no one special. I just do my job and go home. I really don't have anything exciting to share about how I rose to this position. Being in the utility is where the fame is, not serving it!'

With these profiles, my goal is to inspire women (and men) to look seriously at a career serving the utility industry. It only took the Pandemic for me to personally realize not just the sustainability of the business, but the relationships I had built at my two Northeast and New England utility accounts transcended the distance between them and my home in Florida.

It took a few months for people to warm up to the idea of this book, maybe because I didn't really know how to articulate it.

What I learned from the feedback (and most importantly my own thoughts and concerns) is that the more I wrote about these women, the more excited I became. Make no mistake, I am not a great author, but I did find and retain a great editor. I hope this book and these women inspire you to look seriously at this industry. I also hope it inspires you to find your Superpower and your Kryptonite and make them both work to make you a woman of power and utilities.

I thank you for reading this book, and I trust you will be as inspired by these women as I am.

Connie Turner Carden

ACKNOWLEDGEMENTS

The proverb, 'It takes a village to raise a child,' appropriately describes the process of authoring this book; it truly required a collective effort. I am deeply grateful to the nine extraordinary women who entrusted me with their stories, allowing me to chronicle their ventures into the dynamic world of the utility industry. Following the interviews, a dedicated team worked tirelessly behind the scenes, strengthened by the unwavering support of my family and colleagues.

This book has been both a labor of love and sometimes just labor. My husband, Clint, has been a witness to the countless hours spent preparing, conducting, writing and editing each chapter, all while juggling a full-time job and family responsibilities. His support was steadfast; he read only one paragraph to avoid influencing my perspective, ensuring I remained true to my vision. As the publication date drew near, his encouragement and attentive listening were invaluable as I brought the book to completion.

I owe a debt of gratitude to my scribe and friend, Mary Johnson. By day, she is my executive assistant; by night and on weekends, she was instrumental in recording and transcribing the interviews, promptly providing me with the materials needed to quickly write each chapter.

I am honored that my friend of 10 years, Rockie Soloman, agreed to write the Foreword. A woman of deep faith, Rockie has been a beacon of serenity in my life when I needed it most.

My personal editor, Cindy O'Hara, played a crucial role in this endeavor. Writing is not my strong suit, and Cindy worked diligently to refine my skills. Although we may have conceded defeat on punctuation and capitalization by chapter three, her guidance was indispensable.

I extend my thanks to Jordan Torr, a colleague at my firm and a member of this book's target audience. Her work on an SAP project for a major New England utility has the potential to spark a lifelong passion for the industry.

The book's cover, notable for its compelling design, is the creation of Matthew James Riesmeyer, an emerging artist and professional with considerable promise in the fields of creative and graphic design. His generosity in sharing his expertise and dedication has culminated in a cover that is distinguished and extraordinary to all. He can be reached on his LinkedIn profile.

Penni Conner, my longtime friend and executive vice president at Eversource, planted the seed for this book. An accomplished author, writer and speaker, Penni provided invaluable feedback and inspiration throughout this journey. Her support has been instrumental in making this book one of my proudest achievements.

Women of Power and Utilities would not exist without Innovate UtilityCX (IUCX), formerly known as CS Week. IUCX, a non-profit organization, is committed to providing educational opportunities for utilities. Their publishing arm, launched in 2014, has made my publication dreams a reality, and I am proud to be the first author under their rebranded IUCX Aspiring Authors program.

I am grateful to IUCX CEO Rod Litke and his publishing team for the chance to honor these remarkable women. Copy editor Janet Grabinski skillfully brought their stories to life. Lisa Collins managed marketing and printing with expertise, while Jawon Smith ensured our digital presence was felt across social media platforms.

My appreciation extends to the IUCX Board of Directors, particularly Jared Lawrence and Mark Wyatt, whose support was crucial. Their endorsement allowed me to proudly display the IUCX logo on my work.

To Clint, my partner of 29 years: your patience and trust have been the bedrock of this project. Thank you for being my steadfast supporter. To my son, Brandon and his wife, Joslyn: I hope this book offers you insights into my journey and the mentors who have shaped it.

To my adopted family, who have patiently listened to me talk about this book for two years: your encouragement has been a source of strength. Special thanks to Joe Nelms, Jan Caswell,

Robyn Johnson, Danielle Sanzotta, Ada and Mike Ruzinsky, Carl Morton, Tracey and Brian Demarco, Sheila and Teben Pyles, Carol and Vincent Bocelli, Jeffery Lasean Rogers and Scott and Renee DiPatri. Also, to my Boston-adopted family, Penni and Nick Conner, Tito Jackson and Justin Brown: I love that no matter how far away I am, you all make us feel so close!

My work family deserves thanks for their guidance, critiques and good-natured ribbing. Brian Martin, Ryan Levine, Mike Riggins, NicCole Newcomb, Chitra Bose, Mark Hirschey, Christopher Smith, Jake Van Reen, Varun Sharma, Ron Trenouth, Julie McAlary, Kerri Meredith, Jamaal Stanford, Huzaifah Basrai, Kyle Harkrader, Dean Hansen, Greg Guthridge, Craig Crawford, Mehul Shah, Milena Beshkova, Richard Charles, Will Carpenella, Karen Felton, Joy Bell, Tolu Ogunsanya, Lauren Marcellin Bell, Kristen Banks, Stephanie Chesnick, Steve Wanner and many others have contributed to this endeavor.

I would like to extend my sincere gratitude to the leadership of the GridWise Alliance, specifically to its Chief Executive Officer Karen Wayland and Executive Director K. Malaika Walton. Serving on their Board of Directors for four years has been a distinct honor. Their exemplary leadership and profound knowledge of the industry have served as a source of inspiration for me and all women. I commend them for their remarkable achievements and the success they have brought to the organization!

Finally, to all the readers: I hope you find inspiration in these women's stories and gain an appreciation for the sustainability of a career in the utility industry. May you discover your own Superpower - we all have one, waiting to be uncovered.

Please note that I will not receive royalties from this book. My agreements with IUCX Aspiring Authors and my firm preclude secondary income. Proceeds from the sales will benefit a domestic violence shelter in Jacksonville, FL, a personal philanthropic initiative of mine. Your support for this cause is deeply appreciated. Thank you again, and I hope you enjoy this read!

Chapter 1:
What's Her Superpower?

W hen I first began visualizing this book, the purpose was to highlight the industry I love and the women I respect. I also want to attract and retain women, young and old, to a career in the utility industry. However, since I embarked on this journey in mid-2023, my mission has expanded significantly. Being a part of this industry since the early 1980s has allowed me to witness its transformation and the evolution of the women (and men) within it. While I have never been employed by a utility company, I have had the privilege of collaborating closely with those who are. Some of the women featured here began their careers within utilities, but the majority have been or are associated with technology hardware, software or services vendors - those vital firms that develop, sell and implement products to elevate customer experience within the utility industry.

As I conducted interviews, we posed two probing questions: "What is your Superpower?" and "What is your Kryptonite?". Many hesitated to acknowledge their Superpowers - their strengths - yet quickly identified their Kryptonites - their vulnerabilities. 'I struggle with imposter syndrome,' 'I have difficulty saying no,' 'I can't find work-life balance,' 'I assume too much responsibility,' 'I get bored easily;': these were all genuine responses to the Kryptonite query.

> *"No one is you and that is your superpower."*
> **- Brian Ford**

But when asked about Superpowers, the common answer was, 'Let me think about that.' Reflecting on each woman's narrative, I observed commonalities, identifying what I perceived as their Superpowers. Each was shaped by Science, Technology, Engineering and Mathematics (STEM) curricula, sometimes before the acronym itself gained prominence. Each had encountered challenges that invoke their natural resilience and a clear vision of their goals.

> *"Every challenge faced by women in STEM becomes a stepping-stone towards a brighter future, regardless of industry. This is not just for themselves but for generations to come!"*
> **- Hope Utterbeck**, EVP and CIO, Liberty Bank, CT

In Patty Bruffy's case, she stepped into the utility industry during the 1970s, an era dominated by men. She navigated the delicate balance of blending in while staying true to herself. Taking stock of Patty's history, she displays resiliency and a commitment to honesty which defines her Superpowers. Her cape flies when facing daunting challenges or being resolute in her uncompromising honesty, as highlighted in her remembrances of her early career. More of her story lies ahead in Chapter 2.

Debbie Bates's career took off in the 1980s. As an educated and determined Black woman, she initially dismissed the surrounding prejudices. She believed that hard work and perseverance would lead to advancement. However, she later discovered the complexities of corporate progression. With her cape in hand, Debbie demonstrated her true Superpower: agility. When her initial strategy didn't yield the desired results, she reassessed and adapted. Debbie currently holds the esteemed role of senior partner at IBM. Her journey is ahead in Chapter 3.

Lisa A. Dalesandro DiChristofer, a trailblazer in the industry, was one of the earliest female executives amongst men. She self-identifies her Superpower as the nurturing "Italian mother," but in my view, her Superpower extends to persistence. Looking back over my 40 years, Lisa has been steadfast in her dedication to SAP. In her 28-year tenure, she has donned her cape to weather the multitude of changes and challenges within the industry. More about the rewards of loyalty to a single company and its vision are in Chapter 4.

Transcending boundaries, Lakshmi Ravindran's story which begins in the 1990s in India is marked by a global pursuit of knowledge and embodies a zeal for computer science. She sees trustworthiness as her Superpower and rightly so. But from my years of collaborating with her, I've recognized an even greater Superpower: her humility. Lakshmi's extensive knowledge, like her cape, is not obvious but is evident the moment she discusses the SAP product. During projects, while making tough decisions, her calm demeanor provides wisdom and the path forward to resolve issues. Learn more about her zealousness for excellence in Chapter 5.

In the 2000s, Maureen Coveney Bolen started her journey as a nuclear engineer at General Electric. Her route to the utility consulting sector and her varied background voice an intriguing conversation. She perceives her Superpower as being an attentive listener—a true asset. However, I have observed other, greater Superpowers: passion and initiative. While her early years were tough, she donned her cape in college and met those challenges with stamina and determination. Maureen, brilliant and driven, remains grounded and exceedingly approachable. More about her exciting journey is ahead in Chapter 6.

Susan Lynch carved her path in the 1990s from Big 8 accounting and found her niche in utilities. Fortunately for this industry, she has remained. While Susan claims likability as her Superpower, I see her tenacity as her defining force. Once she commits, her cape is on and does not waver. There is no turning back. Her story underscores the importance of trusting oneself and leaning in on your gut instincts. More about Susan is shared in Chapter 7.

Michelle Fay's foresight led her to obtain degrees in computer science and accounting in the 2000s. She leveraged her education from the start, positioning herself as a subject matter expert in a technical field. Michelle sees her Superpower as building teams, a skill I've witnessed since meeting her in 2002. Observing her ascent in the utility consulting market, I see Michelle's Superpower as her enthusiasm to embrace change. Michelle dons her cape in the face of trials and dives in to fully understand the challenges and lead others. Michelle embraced challenges ahead of her time, a lesson I hope all women will take to heart: "You don't need to have all the answers to try something new!" Michelle's story is one of courage. Read more about her enterprising approach in Chapter 8.

Beth Kearns emerged in the 1990s with a clear path towards success. She donned her cape in her early years, when she determined she could be the chief executive officer of her own firm. She describes her Superpower as persistence, a trait omnipresent in building her company. Nevertheless, it is her attention to detail, reliability and extreme ownership in honoring commitments that set her apart, as demonstrated when she meticulously reviewed her chapter. Read more about her experience becoming an entrepreneur in her Chapter 9 profile.

Laura Sciuto represents the future, the young talent essential for the industry's ongoing transformation. Shifting from a 'brat' to a 'swan,' Laura is one of my most accomplished mentees. Her cape is proudly displayed to everyone she meets, as she is the person with the vision and the one who 'gets things done.' While she touts decision-making as her Superpower, I'd argue her Superpower is her vision for innovation that truly sets her apart. She is always thinking a step ahead to ensure today's actions yield tomorrow's desired outcomes. Laura's story is still being written, but her tremendous beginning is told in Chapter 10.

My own story is told in Chapter 11. There, I look back on those who have most influenced me. I have been very fortunate to grow and learn from each of these women and they from me. I share some lessons learned on my career journey.

Each woman's story in this collection reveals various paths leading to a shared destination: a fulfilling career serving the utility industry while forming lifetime clients and sustaining longstanding friendships.

As you delve into each story, you'll ponder their Superpowers — what uniquely equips them to excel in this field. In the end, rather than assigning labels, the book invites you to reflect on their journeys and the broader context of each woman's strength within the industry.

And I invite you to find your own Superpower!

"Being a woman itself is a superpower." — Unknown

Chapter 2:
Patty Bruffy
Retired Managing Director at a
Big Four Accounting Firm

F *rom the Author:*

I met Patty Bruffy while I was at IBM in early 2012. At the time, she was working as an Advanced Metering Infrastructure Subject Matter Expert (SME) at a utility client in Florida. Patty is witty and fun; however, she is competent and brilliant in her knowledge of utility operations, as well as meter-to-cash systems. She works harder than most, and no matter the client she served or the leadership level she attained, she always looked out for the clients' best interest.

I watched her at IBM and later at my current company, and she continued to inspire me. In fact, Patty is the primary reason for this book. For more than 40 years, she worked diligently for her clients but always remembered her roots as a utility employee. She was modest in her approach, but by the end of the conversation with a client, there was no misunderstanding of the value she could and would bring to their company and their projects.

I watched her grow and face many challenges; she never gave up or in. I have also witnessed many successes, such as closing big deals and being promoted to managing director. She retired in 2021 without fanfare or a gold watch after 40 years of serving this industry. It is her quiet elegance that demanded that she be included in this book. I hope you can glean a sliver of the brilliance and excellence she brought to my professional career and personal growth. – C.T.C.

Leadership and Personal Work History

Patty started her career out of college with the Executive Office of the President of the United States, Washington, DC Telecommunications Policy in 1976, as administration support. She acquired security clearance and a career in politics but realized she didn't have political aspirations.

While in the White House, she heard about a job within the utility industry at Potomac Electric Power Company (PEPCO). She interviewed and got the job. When she started, she was responsible for the budgeting process and supported rate case filings. She became intrigued with rate case research and supported many senior executives with prepping for testimony hearings. At this time, she married and put in place a plan to move to a more sustainable career.

Because of her outstanding work ethic demonstrated in rate filings, a peer colleague approached Patty for another position in the utility control center. She applied for and received a job as a communications representative and was responsible for streamlining operations status information to the call center, media relations and other operating areas of the company. And this is where it all started. Patty became the first female management employee in the distribution operations area at a 24-hour control center hub of the company, complete with a beeper.

She had to quickly understand not only the job but how to find acceptance from her operations team. She learned to get her job done by respecting their experience working under pressure and gathering information under rapidly changing conditions. She experienced that when a crisis hit everyone should be working toward a common goal, and people in various departments must communicate effectively or service would suffer. She worked storms that ranged from one night to several days and required her to sleep at her desk or pull chairs together for a makeshift bed. She developed an emergency response plan to bring into play factors such as operation plans, event escalation and internal/external coordination triggers to get people and systems working cooperatively. It took a lot of buy-in, training and drills.

After proving her worth to the operations center, she quickly moved through the ranks to senior, then to manager in communications and performance, and to manager of the engineering group that supported the control group where she first started.

Due to personal circumstances, her family had to move to Georgia. At some time in a woman's career, she must decide between her family and her career. Patty planned to do both, so she built a plan and executed it. At that time, it took real courage, but she did it.

Her initial project was as a subcontractor to a small consulting firm. She built upon her emergency response experience learned at the utility and implemented a dress rehearsal drill with more than 325 employees and an incident command center for Y2K, otherwise known as Year 2000.

After she completed the Year 2000 projects, Patty decided to dedicate herself to consulting in the utility industry. Her previous job with PEPCO had exposed her to functional work, project management, IT innovation and process improvement. It was then that she started her own consulting business, PRB Consulting (2001-2005) and again subcontracted back to her old utility. While there, she cultivated numerous vendor relationships which catapulted her into the vendor community.

Subsequently, she established herself with a small boutique firm which concentrated solely on serving the utility community. She accepted an offer as the vice president of business change management, with responsibility for change management methodology, process evaluation, resolution of process performance issues, outage management, training in outage management and assessment of processes that could benefit from enhanced system integration.

The next phase of her consulting career was at one of the top hardware, software and consulting services firms, IBM, where she worked from 2005-2015. She began as a senior managing consultant with Global Business Services in Strategy and Analytics. It was there that she managed even larger transformational projects, including her own utilization, her teams' and that of sales.

Her last phase in the workforce was with another Big Four consulting firm where she spent six years until her retirement in January 2021. Patty took an initial step back in rank and became a senior manager in the Enterprise Asset Management team and then was quickly promoted to managing director. After winning and delivering numerous large projects nationwide, she stayed through the initial COVID Pandemic challenges. Afterward, with a more than 40-year career to stand on, she finally decided that retirement was in order, so she could dedicate more time to her family.

Career Foundation

Patty's career foundation was built by peers and operations colleagues who shared knowledge about the utility industry when she walked into an organization at an entry management level as a female. They instilled in her the importance of the services provided to get the lights back on in an outage, maintaining the system and knowing the people and the operations of the business.

She immediately learned that teamwork was under pressure when she worked her first storm, learning how to be in the middle of operators and the thousands of questions bombarding them in just hours. Her job was to gather operating information without being bothersome. Mentoring was not a customary practice when Patty started her career in the 1970s. She realized quickly that she had to network across the operating areas, get buy-in for changes and know when to ask for help.

As she progressed in her career, learning to 'team-under-fire' benefited her in many ways. As a vendor, one does not often get to select one's consultants. Mostly, people are assigned to one's project because it needs to be staffed for billable hours, and it is because of those staffing challenges that everyone needs to be adaptive.

Patty always found time to offer advice especially when it comes to assisting people as they build their career foundation. Below are a few points that helped her over the years:

1. Learn how to **provide stability** to your team while facing extreme client pressure. Even if they are new to you and your project, you need to be available to know them as a professional and a person.

o **Recognize every member**. The best solutions come from partnership so encourage input.

o **Communicate.** Meetings must communicate status frequently. Each project may have a distinctive style. The best-case example was when Patty had teams working in multiple states. This unit had a short Monday kick-off and then a detailed Wednesday review of each team's progress, issues and shared concerns. The client commented, 'She and her team knew more about their organization and what to do than any of their leaders.'

o **Develop and know how to leverage the team's skills**. Know which roles to task your staff. When under stress, assess whether you have your people in the right roles, coach them, but move personnel right away with the understanding that it's to help everyone involved.

o **Trust your staff when the stakes are high, and the pressure is on**. Many leaders don't do this and step over their workers or talk over them which can lead the team to shut down.

2. **Allow others to shine**. Make sure that you always remember that it's about the team and the individuals.

o **Thank them**. These two simple words, either personally or on conference calls, will go a long way to getting everyone on board.

o **Advocate for your team**. Letting management and executives know about staff performance and inviting leadership to meet the team at the site/meetings will help everyone feel empowered.

o **Promote and develop them**. Give personnel key roles at presentations and meetings. Offer team members more career training.

o **Recognize team members to leadership**. Give them opportunities to shine.

3. **Always stand your truth**.

   o **Stand up for yourself**. There is no position that is more important than integrity. The definition of right is not the same for everyone.

   o **Make the hard call**. Pressure came to Patty once on repeated calls with veiled consequences to make a client sale that she knew the client didn't need. She chose not to push the client and took the internal hit. It was the right decision for many reasons for the company and the client. A year later that client found out, and she enjoyed a stronger relationship for making a call against the firm's wishes.

   o **Defend your team**. Patty had employees that the company wanted to fire, and she stood up based on performance reviews. Sometimes reviews aren't based on all the facts. You must lead behind the scenes if you know it's the right thing to do.

"Experience teaches you how to stand your truth!" - **Patty Bruffy**

Developing Exceptional Client Service as a Team

Patty has had many years of talent development and is known by past employees for her passion for identifying and molding great consultants. One thing she notices immediately is the candidate's capability to communicate with her in the interview and later with the client. Just because one may identify skills as a SME in a particular area doesn't innately make that person an effective communicator.

Do you possess critical thinking skills without direction? Can you collaborate across different areas? Can you demonstrate your flexibility? Patty's message was always the same. "How can you demonstrate your knowledge? Because it's not a source of power if you can't share it."

Patty had specific attributes when looking for new consultants. Even though she started recruiting consultants in the late '70s, the process for hiring remains the same:

o Can the candidate communicate clearly, empathetically and with confidence? Since consultants are hired as SMEs, the ability to deliver written and verbal messages is critical to success. In the utility industry, it is difficult to hide your lack of knowledge. It's better to say, "I don't know."

o Can the candidate demonstrate that they can problem-solve? Can they solve and work independently, or will they need constant supervision?

o Does the candidate show collaboration? Development of a collaborative relationship with peers and clients is imperative to being a great consultant. Working well with others not only strengthens skills, but it also allows for growth.

o Are they good listeners? Listening to and understanding the client's problem is paramount to being a good consultant. Without great listening skills, one cannot begin to advise on what needs solving.

One characteristic that helped Patty recruit and retain staff was her capacity to build and live her culture. She fostered an inclusive environment and made sure all staff felt heard and acknowledged. She made sure people understood how they were organized both internally and externally to the client. Organization is about how people relate to each other when engaged in joint endeavors. Managing and maintaining a project-specific organization is important in project delivery, especially at the very beginning, so everyone understands their individual role and how they should behave as a team.

Once Patty had her team identified, culture-engrained and projects underway, she concentrated on making sure that she retained the talent she had so carefully selected and nurtured. She was a huge fan of mentoring programs both within her own staff and externally to those that reached out to her for coaching. When she was with larger systems integrators, formally structured mentoring programs were in place, but even as she progressed in her career in smaller firms, Patty employed informal mentoring processes. In addition to her day job, and because it was important to her, she spent time ensuring her staff was well-cared for. This quality is a part of why she was a tremendous leader and why she had successful projects.

Building a Brand

Since Patty began her career more than four decades ago, things have changed. When she first started in the '70s, women were told they had to act like men to get ahead, and it reflected in women's dress. There wasn't much feminine touch or style to work with, and women's suits were demanded for client presentations. At one company, Patty was approached by a young team member who asked if she had to wear panty hose. The answer was yes because it was expected. Times were quite different then, and those dressing rules were adopted by many women in the '70s, but that wasn't Patty's personality, so she remained resilient in all changing conditions. Working in utility operations taught her to 'weather the storm.' There was a perception (correct or not) that leaders of this era were more likely to promote people in their own likeness. Women also feared the judgment that having children would hinder careers or impact raises. Daycare was also hard to find and manage; Patty had to have multiple back-up plans to care for her children while at work.

She built her career in the trench's operations experience. She leveraged distribution, transmission, control room operations and emergency management with process and project management. Her years in real-time operations started with studying paper circuitry maps and operator reports. As technology emerged, it helped her to work 'the big picture' with clients. She also expanded all her operations knowledge to training operators and used this experience to work on change management projects. She felt it was important to connect people to processes. Those connections across the project were key to her success.

Her brand combined vendor project management and real-time experience in that she could step back and see both sides of solving a problem. In her industry, she had seen what worked and what didn't, using consultants. She lived in the utility era of changing many paper-based processes to innovative technology. The biggest lesson she learned was how to listen to the client and know what specific problem needed to be solved.

Now that women are in every area of utility operations, customer call centers and information technology, they each carry and apply their own style. Women are being hired into historically male dominated positions. Pay gaps have narrowed, more positions are available, and women are leading. Women have come a long way, but there is still a long way to go.

Patty has many Superpowers, but upon reflection she is the best advisor on any subject in the utility space, from customer to operations. She is always a wealth of knowledge, and even when asked the most basic question her response is kind and thoughtful. Patty has only one Kryptonite: her inability to say, "No." There have been many times where she was up all night because she committed to a client or coworker a deliverable that required more hours than in a day.

Patty's Brand Attributes

- ❖ Resiliency
- ❖ Adaptability
- ❖ Capacity to Problem Solve
- ❖ Connecting Clients to Solutions
- ❖ Recognition of Strong Women

Final Thoughts

Patty's story is one of much wisdom. The best leaders are humble and strong communicators, and whether you are a utility professional or a vendor serving a utility client, communication is the key to success. Raise your hand when you need help. Show up. Use your talents. Keep faith and keep moving forward. Ask yourself frequently: Am I using my talents for the right thing? Patty wishes her legacy to be one of breaking down barriers and paving a way for women, regardless of industry, to know that they can be effective. It just takes patience, but mostly it takes heart! In her words, "You really don't have to be loud to be strong; you need to be fierce."

"Throughout the time I've known Patty, she is someone who consistently demonstrates exceptional leadership skills while also standing out for her remarkable level of personal care and human connection. She has a natural ability to inspire and guide others, setting a high standard for teamwork and performance. Whether it was navigating challenging projects or motivating team members, she always exhibited strong leadership. What truly sets Patty apart is her genuine empathy and personable approach. Beyond her extensive professional expertise, she genuinely cares about the well-being of her colleagues and the success of the team. She always goes above and beyond to foster a supportive and collaborative environment, making everyone feel valued and heard. Patty's unique combination of leadership and genuine empathy really made an impact on my professional and personal growth." - **Sean Clark-McCarthy, Manager, Enterprise Asset Management**
Collaborated directly with her at EY, LLP

Chapter Highlights   Description

Career Beginnings

Started in the '70s, a time when women were expected to emulate men in the workplace.

Resilience

Remained resilient despite changing conditions and workplace expectations.

Operational Expertise

Built career with hands-on experience in utility operations, including emergency management.

Technological Adaptation

Transitioned from paper-based processes to embracing and implementing innovative technology.

Problem-Solving Approach

Known for listening to clients and understanding their specific problems to find solutions.

Industry Evolution	Witnesses and contributed to the significant changes in the utilities industry for women.
Superpower	Being an exceptional advisor with a wealth of knowledge in all aspects of the utility space.
Kryptonite	Inability to say "no," leading to overcommitment and working extra hours to meet obligations.
Leadership and Training	Used operational knowledge to train operators and work on change management projects.
Client and Process Connection	Emphasized the importance of connecting people to processes for project success.
Women's Progress in Utilities	Acknowledges the strides made by women in the industry and the journey ahead.

Patty, a native Virginian, attended James Madison University earning a degree in Business Administration. Currently retired, she and her husband, Jim, live in West Florida where they enjoy time with her family both in the U.S. and in England. Additional information about Patty can be found on LinkedIn at https://www.linkedin.com/in/1pattybruffy/

Chapter 3:
Debbie Bates
Senior Partner at IBM

F rom the Author:

In 2011, I joined IBM as a partner in their Oracle practice. Debbie worked in that same practice as a delivery consultant for Oracle Enterprise Relationship Planning (ERP). I was hired to sell and deliver work for all things Oracle, primarily Oracle Customer Care and Billing, a Customer Information System (CIS). Unknown to me on my hire date, there was another woman partner, already with tenure, who was in line for the same national job. Unfortunately, that caused my team and me conflict from the first day.

My first sales opportunity was with NiSource Gas in Columbus, OH. The project entailed a total transformation of their ERP and CIS with Oracle, and the IBM team led by me prepared for our client presentation.

Debbie Bates, another 10 to 12 IBM consultants and I were part of the client presentation team, along with the partner who was overlooked for promotion. Things deteriorated quickly. Since she was the senior partner and I the junior, she had seniority. Each day we prepared, the senior partner became more combative, and each day I cowered more at the sound of her voice.

One Thursday afternoon at the Columbus airport, Debbie and I were waiting for flights back to our respective homes. Grief, sadness and depression overwhelmed me. I was miserable, and *after a grueling week of work I could no longer keep my composure. Debbie listened as I lamented about the situation, almost inconsolable from my anguish. It was then that she offered me a handkerchief. Debbie didn't know me at all. The truth was that she was merely an observer in a war that I was never going to win, but she still handed me that gift that belonged to her mother. It was that day that I made a friend for life.*

When I think of exceptional women in the industry, I immediately think of Debbie. She is profiled in this book because of the outstanding contribution she has made professionally but also because of the impact she has made on my life.

Her journey to partner at IBM was one of victories and defeats, each molding her to be the role model she has become. She exemplifies everything that I admire, and her story is my pleasure to share. – C.T.C.

Leadership and Personal Work History

To say that Debbie Bates is an intelligent person who happens to be a woman would be an understatement. She grew up in New York City to two engaged parents, and I was privileged enough to meet her father, Albert Williams. Growing up, Debbie's only mentors were her parents. Hers was not an environment where she saw people such as herself in leadership roles in business. She attended private schools in the City, graduated high school in three years and then went on to New York University, again graduating in three years with a Bachelor of Arts, Liberal Arts and Sciences/Liberal Studies in 1978.

Eager to see what was outside of NYC, she moved to San Francisco where she attended the University of San Francisco, attaining a Master of Business Administration in Finance, Finance General, in collaboration with Fireman's Fund Insurance Company. After graduation, she landed a job immediately as a director of information management business planning at that same firm.

It was not long before she was homesick for the Northeast and moved back to New York City and joined the KPMG team in 1998. While there, she worked in several industries - insurance, banking and finally utilities for 10 years. It was at that time that KPMG became KPMG Consulting as KPMG wanted to separate their audit practice and allow KPMG Consulting to become a public company. After two years, KPMG Consulting became a publicly traded company rebranded as BearingPoint. When Debbie first joined KPMG, the firm felt smaller. She didn't want to continue at a public company, so she looked at other options.

She left and joined Genpact and travelled the world, consulting in India as well as Ireland, Europe and Canada. She spent five years with Genpact and determined there was too little work-life balance.

After leaving Genpact, she interviewed and accepted a job with IBM in the utility practice, and that is where we met. However, she recognized early in her tenure at IBM the lack of women in consulting and more importantly the lack of women in leadership roles, specifically in the utilities industry. She also saw that situation across the firm, not just in that sector. She made a goal as she began her career there: to make sure women were mentored for leadership roles and see that they had to chance to get them.

Debbie's experience with financial services and regulated industries provided her the opportunity to collaborate with many outstanding companies: Southern Company in Atlanta, GA; Oncor in Dallas, TX; NiSource in Columbus, OH; Ameren in St. Louis, MO are just some of the marquee clients where she continued gathering industry knowledge and consulting savvy.

As she gained more knowledge and confidence, she moved away from the investor-owned utilities and on to state and local markets, which she embraced because she felt her work had influence and impacted her clients and the communities served. She gained an affinity for serving people and seeing the software she sold and implemented change constituents' lives. Implementing social security systems, customer relationship management and state portals that helped people with their daily lives were just a few of the meaningful projects that provided Debbie fulfillment.

Debbie continues her work at IBM but has moved on to a global role. In her current position, she supports many time zones and cultures. She continues to grow as a professional but still remembers how she began her career and the foundation she built when she started. Quite a lot has changed over her career, but fostering women to embrace industry, especially those that were once male dominated, is a lifelong ambition.

Career Foundation

When Debbie launched her career, there were few women in the industry, especially women of color. Her foundation has been built on intelligence, hard work and ingenuity, and she has spent every day making sure that her footing was sound. As she continued her journey, she began to build her team's culture on openness and a celebration of differences. She wanted to create a space where women felt comfortable to stand on their own and be protected. When she collaborated with young women, even today, she wants them to feel that they have a voice, feel important, secure and see advancement in their careers.

When it comes to pressure, Debbie feels as if women's are self-imposed. Poor planning and lack of preparedness on our part, she believes, causes anxiety that could be avoided.

When building her foundation, she never dreamed she would end her career in a global role. Debbie spends a lot of her personal time travelling the world, visiting every country she can (her last visit was to Jordan), but when it came to leading a worldwide organization at IBM, this wasn't in the plan.

At IBM, she was tapped to run a post-implementation services organization where she was the leader in transforming major systems and their application and cloud support. That means around-the-world support and communication. However, she has excelled in this role. Her years of experience have taught her this: you need to create an atmosphere where people feel heard. She creates an environment where everyone has a voice and knows that their feedback is sought after and incorporated into the decision-making process.

> *"Debbie exemplifies the qualities that make an implementation partner successful, a problem-solving mentality, an empathy with the client and a tireless level of engagement in the important details without losing sight of the big picture."* **- Wael Hibri, SVP, Shared Services and later Deputy Chief Transformation Officer**

As she reflected during our interview, Debbie had managers who recognized and rewarded her work, but they didn't coach or develop her, and they certainly weren't champions. Like many women then and now, any role or promotion she received was because she was already performing the work for several years before she got the promotion and the pay that accompanied it. She never got that 'stretch' opportunity or the benefit of the doubt that she could grow quickly into a role. There is a real difference between supporting people and mentoring people. She seldom had someone help her make those critical career choices or someone who floated her name as opportunities presented themselves, not in her current role or in previous positions. As a direct result, she feels a need to promote women and lead campaigns on their behalf, move them into opportunities where they can thrive and build those connections for promotions and career advancement.

When you meet Debbie, she is hard to read. She is a heads-down person and certainly not a broker of relationships. In reference to herself, she will say that it has been challenging to get connected, and without the advice of others or asking for that assistance, she would not be as successful in life and in work as she has become. It takes real bravery to know your skills and exceptional courage to know your shortcomings.

What does she tell her mentees? BE BOLD! When women (and even men) are new to their positions, they tend to be hesitant and need validation for their viewpoints. You don't lose by being bold! If there is an adjustment that needs to be made, the sooner you course correct the better. Do not be hesitant. Debbie also advises to do your research, get your facts and form your opinions. When you're invited to a meeting, you have a chair at the table so use it. If you do not have an opinion and can't add value, decline the meeting.

Developing Exceptional Client Service - Team Development

Debbie has always been known as an exceptional leader among her peers and when asked to share their thoughts about her leadership, colleagues across many companies came forward with comments including this one:

> *"I have a deep respect and admiration for Debbie Bates that has only grown in the almost 15 years since we initially became colleagues. She is the epitome of a Servant Leader, which shines throughout her engagement with IBM clients, and in paying forward, her expertise to mentor and nurture junior staff.*
> *As Debbie has taken on broader strategic roles at IBM and grown the business, her influence has expanded to also grow the next generation of women and minority leaders in technology — a legacy to balance and diversify the technology workforce for the future."*
> **- Kathleen (Kathi) Hanrahan, Women in Technology (WIT) Board Member, Executive Committee Secretary**

When asked about managing adversity, either from other women or men, Debbie's answer was simple: "I just moved on. You must think: 'Do you want to die on this hill?' Consider how much this decision will matter in the future. All decisions may impact the future, but some have much longer lasting effects whether it's personal or professional."

However, on a few occasions, she did report to Human Resources when she felt there was blatant bias or discrimination regarding how she was addressed and treated. "If you do not feel I or a member of my team provide the level of service quality and you want to move us out, you have that right. But you must do that with respect. I will not allow myself or my team to be spoken down to." When you see something wrong, you have an obligation to stand up and speak the truth. Debbie follows this quote:

> *"A wise woman wishes to be no one's enemy; a wise woman refuses to be anyone's victim."* **– Maya Angelou**

Failing as a leader is not a new concept, but how you manage it is either a defining moment or a lifetime regret. Debbie failed once, and she thinks she did not ever really recover. Like many women, she minimizes her successes and embraces her failures. She advises to "shake it off" as it is one thing to learn from a mistake and quite another to let it weigh you down. One failure she regrets was not remaining on a project to completion - the only project she never finished because it was too transactional and not solution-oriented. Reflecting, she learned that she should have identified the problem early and worked to resolve it. According to Debbie: Retract yourself quickly and treat it as a learning experience.

When building her team, her instinct is to choose people like herself: decisive, quick thinkers and meticulous individuals. But she also knows she needs people who think differently than she does, even when it's painful. Teams need people who make us pause and think, and as leaders we need people who harbor a contrarian view to round us out. When initially building a team, we need balance with both right-brained people with integrity and left-brained people who demonstrate deep honesty. We also need to build diverse teams with different life experiences, skill sets and those who operate on multiple dimensions. When a mistake is made, you (or your team members) must own it, learn from it and move on. The decisions we make are ours, and sometimes they're the wrong ones.

Another team building exercise that helps develop her staff is continuous learning. Because things are changing so quickly these days, we need to be as forward (or more forward) thinking than our clients, or we'll add no value to them and be outdated. Every day she asks her team, "What did you learn today?" If it's nothing, then that day has been wasted. To further live by example, she often shares books with her staff that will help continue their personal growth and development. Four of her recent favorites are:

- *Forged in Crisis: The Making of Five Courageous Leaders* by Nancy Koehn
- *Leading Quietly* by Joseph L. Badaracco Jr.
- *Lift as I Climb: An Immigrant Girl's Journey Through Corporate America* by Jackie Glenn
- *What Got You Here Won't Get You There* by Marshall Goldsmith

Once her team completes those readings, they often share them with their client teams. When clients and consultants work as one, understanding the fundamentals of being on a high performing team, projects are more likely to be productive, and everyone can enjoy that success.

Building a Brand

When Debbie began her career, the thought of building a brand wasn't part of her narrative. No one ever explained the value or necessity to her. In hindsight, she did but not in those terms. She wanted to be thought of as an individual who could be relied upon to do the most difficult tasks. She wanted to be the point of reference. If there was a problem, she wanted to be thought of as extremely competent and trustworthy to make the right decision.

However, when others are asked about her brand, the adjectives are plentiful. Debbie is described as reliable and dependable. She is trustworthy and immediately called upon when a client needs a complex project implemented, specifically any Oracle product within the State and Local vertical. She delivers easy and difficult messages well and is transparent about what needs to be accomplished. She has deep expertise. When she speaks, clients are at ease that the project is under control.

Reflecting, she acknowledges that as an African American woman she had to prove that she didn't get her position and role because of minority-based goals or affirmative action. That meant she had to be extremely competent in what she did and in every word she spoke. As she progressed in her career, she realized quickly that her skills were primarily technical, and she did not hone her leadership skills until her move into management roles. She learned quickly that while she had the technical skills needed to do the job, she lacked coaching on how to be a leader and how to collaborate. Then in 2015, she paused. She complemented her technical skills by doubling down on her leadership skills particularly in collaboration and teamwork. She received fair and unbiased feedback and a promotion. She moved her career forward, but she had to step back and take the pulse of the world around her. According to Debbie, it's never too late to reassess where you are and where you want to go.

Debbie's self-assessment of her Superpower is her strength with flexibility. Like Elastagirl, she can bend and adjust when needed, but she doesn't lose sight of her North Star. Debbie confesses that her Kryptonite is that she is opinionated. Building teams when you are strong-willed is challenging. She must make sure she doesn't lead the discussions and form the opinions of others, as that can be the very element that shuts people down and reduces collaboration.

Debbie's advice to all, regardless of age or sex, is to build your brand on passion. She has genuinely enjoyed every job she's had, and her passion has made her good at it. People come out of school with high GPAs and volunteer hours, but did they enjoy the journey? As your passion changes, your brand will naturally evolve around you.

> ## Debbie's Brand Attributes
>
> ❖ Reliable
> ❖ Collaborative
> ❖ Reflective
> ❖ Passionate
> ❖ Competent

Final Thoughts

Looking back at a remarkably successful career, Debbie is excited that her legacy is about to begin. What does she want to leave after her departure? "I would like to think I have made a difference. That when I am no longer doing this work, there is a void."

Not to say that there will be a crash, but when Debbie leaves this space, people will notice that she isn't around anymore. She spent decades creating a work environment where people could thrive and contribute, find joy in their 12 to 14-hour days and enjoy collaborating with her.

Were there things she would have done differently? There always will have been a 'could have, should have,' but she admits early in her career she wasn't focused. She really didn't have a vision map. She had extremely broad experience and opportunities that presented themselves, and she took them as they became available. She worked in numerous countries and travelled the world. She reflects that because her path was not clearly laid out, it took longer to progress in her career than others. "I could have done things differently. But would it have been as enjoyable? Probably not."

As Debbie finished this interview, she provided a last thought that she wanted the reader to reflect on:

> *"I've learned that people will forget what you said, people will forget what you did, but people will never forget how you made them feel."* - **Maya Angelou**

Chapter Highlights	Description
Initial Career Perspective	Did not focus on building a brand but aimed to be reliable and competent in tackling challenges.
External Perception	Known as reliable, dependable and an expert in implementing complex Oracle projects.
Professional Competence	Recognized for deep expertise, trustworthiness and ability to put clients at ease.
Overcoming Stereotypes	Faced the challenge of proving her worth beyond minority-based goals or affirmative action.
Leadership Development	Enhanced leadership skills in collaboration and teamwork, leading to career advancement.
Superpower	Strength with flexibility, able to adapt while staying focused on her goals.
Kryptonite	Being opinionated which can challenge team building and collaboration.

Career Advancement	Stepped back to reassess and move forward, highlighting the importance of continuous self-evaluation.
Advice on Brand Building	Encourages building a brand based on passion, which allows for natural evolution and success.

Debbie lives in Atlanta, GA and loves to travel the globe in her time off. She is a trusted friend to many people around the world. She holds a personal ambition to visit all the Presidential libraries, and she has almost achieved that goal as of this publish date.

More information about Debbie can be found at LinkedIn: https://www.linkedin.com/in/debbie-bates-69518578/

Chapter 4:
Lisa Dalesandro DiChristofer
National Vice President, Head of North America Industry Executive Advisory at SAP

F*rom the Author:*

I met Lisa in 2004 at my first CS Week Women in Utilities forum. SAP and AAC sponsored the initial event which was lightly attended, not because it wasn't lovely but because the utility industry had very few women at that point in history.

I remember meeting Lisa for the first time. She was extremely professional, and she had a presence. She had an air of sophistication, yet she was approachable and certainly knew most people in the room. She delivered a great speech and afterward spent a few minutes with me.

I was known then as 'just a sales representative,' and she was intimidating to me. That day she motivated me to be more, and I decided then that I wanted a new career path.

I have watched her career progression over the last 20 years as she reached the top of her game. During her years at SAP and as the tech industry has evolved, she has faced many challenges but has also learned how to adapt to change and reaped many rewards. Her career story is one to tell and as a woman to emulate. It is for that reason and many more that she is profiled in this book.
– C.T.C.

Learning and Personal Work History

Lisa's entry into the utility industry did not follow a typical path since she wasn't thinking about a career. Her early aspirations were to marry and start a family. She attended college on early admission at a small local area school so she could get a jump start on her plan. She married, started a family and was a stay-at-home mom. However, two short years later, she found herself divorced and a single parent in her early twenties.

This was not what she had planned, and she found herself at a crossroads in need of hitting the reset button. Lisa was encouraged by her family to return to college, and she was accepted to Rutgers State University. She worked evenings and weekends to make ends meet and focused on completing her education and raising her son. She had many jobs during this time including as a call center agent, server, bookkeeper, credit analyst and even performed billing for a law firm. After six years, she graduated college with a Bachelor of Arts in Business Administration.

Lisa had several internships including one with Automation Data Processing (ADP). After graduating, she convinced the recruiter and sales director to hire her as a payroll processing platform salesperson in 1989. This was an old-fashioned door-to-door, foot canvassing sales position. An adaptive person, Lisa quickly became a success. During this time, she returned to college to get her master's degree.

In 1996, SAP, a German software company, was launching its presence in the States and hiring business consultants to sell Enterprise Resource Planning (ERP) software on a new technology called client-server. She joined SAP in 1996 as North America's second woman account executive. She was fortunate to work for two great managers, Bob Salvucci and Jim Surber, who told her, "Go sell some software and try to stay in the United States. And if you go outside the United States, you can't take the Concord." They gave her great coaching and advice and helped her buy her first set of golf clubs and BMW Z3.

SAP was in start-up mode when they entered the States, but the experience Lisa gained while at ADP set her up for success. During her first years at SAP, Lisa worked on several utility accounts. She was drawn to the industry because of the people, the culture and the business opportunities the industry was experiencing. She decided to focus solely on this vertical as an industry account executive. She was promoted to director for about a year where she moved from an individual contributor and further away from field work. However, she missed the field and asked to return to her real joy, supporting her amazing customers. SAP was experiencing a huge surge in business due to Y2K, the internet and the dotcom era. Also, being a single mom, Lisa wanted to take a step back from being a leader to focus on her son. Being a sales director in a software company has many demands and responsibilities. As an individual contributor, she had much more control over her own calendar.

In 2003, she returned to the ranks at SAP as the vice president of utilities and for the next 21 years held various leadership positions within the company, serving both regulated and unregulated utility clients. Her leadership and dedication to the utility industry and her capabilities to support many additional sectors, allowed personal and professional growth. Lisa by then had left her utilities role and was promoted to national vice president and head of SAP's North America Industry Advisory practice for all industries, a role she currently holds.

Career Foundation

When Lisa was starting her journey in life, she was like most of us in the '70s. The last thing on our minds was building a career. Some things early in life you don't consciously think about, you just do.

> **"Don't think, just do!" - *Top Gun's* Maverick**

She reflects that she did not necessarily think about a career foundation, but she had self-awareness and asked herself if what she was doing was relevant and effective.

"I've got a terrible poker face," says Lisa. "If I don't know something, you will be the first to know." Lisa loved working with people and helping them solve their business problems. Early in her career she learned that building lasting relationships with every contact she made - a prospect, a customer or even a competitor - was a foundational aspect of the professional she wanted to become. She always treated people with respect and made sure her interactions with everyone were positive. The industry may be large, but the community is small so you must have integrity and perform with great delivery. Having a technical background with a pleasant personality made her a high-performing, technical sales professional early in her career.

One of Lisa's first customers was Elizabethtown Water in Elizabethtown, PA. It was there that Lisa met Nellie Jefferson. Nellie was new in her role as a director and anxious to make sure she was successful. It was a first project for both Lisa and Nellie. They formed a bond and shared a commitment to deliver a quality SAP project. Fortunately, they had guidance and mentorship from Bruce Hawthorne. He taught them how to manage complex IT projects, develop effective change management and communication skills and solve business problems with technology.

During this time, Lisa also met other influential women in the utility industry. One that stands out is Kathy Sanders, a senior partner at Accenture. Kathy may not have known it, but she was a great role model for Lisa at a time when there were few women in the industry unless they were serving coffee.

In the late 1990s, there were three other women at SAP - Karen Rogers, Cathy Tough and Amy Phelps - who were also committed to this amazing industry. They worked together, and in the early days they were like a sisterhood. Lisa claims this is one of the reasons why she has stayed at SAP for so long. The people and the culture are vibrant, and everyone shares in the wins and the losses. The utility industry is a small community, and everyone at SAP watches after each other like family.

> *"You only have one chance to prove yourself, so you better do good business: always maintain the highest integrity of your relationships." - Lisa A. Dalesandro DiChristofer*

Lisa has maintained a long, successful career and has been with SAP for 28 years which has stood the test of time. There are few people, much less women, who have achieved the longevity of a fruitful relationship with a large enterprise software company.

Delivering Exceptional Client Service – Team Development

In developing exceptional client service, you must begin with a strong team and culture. Creating high performance culture, where teams deliver on expectations, encourages accountability, clear roles and responsibilities and treating people as you would want to be treated.

Over her 28 years, Lisa has been influenced by many great leaders and one or two subpar ones that have helped her become the leader she is today. Developing one-on-one relationships with people on teams is paramount in building consensus. Assembling teams of people with diverse backgrounds and thoughts always produces the best result.

Lisa describes herself as a transparent leader who sets clear objectives and measures success based on results. "The work we do is not a 'spectator sport;' you've got to do the pick-and-shovel work, but you can also have some fun too."

Managing strong client and consultant relationships over the years at SAP has been a cornerstone of her success. Lisa reflected at the beginning of her career that she was not the most experienced person in the room, but she always wanted to be smart and prepared. Who was she meeting with? What's the problem to solve? What research did I already prepare? What is the purpose of the meeting? If those questions can't be answered, then there shouldn't be a meeting. Always be flexible. Good brand ambassadors are always agile and ready for anything, even if it's not on their agenda.

Building a Brand

When Lisa was at ADP, they used to have 'roll calls' each Tuesday night where each sales rep had to stand up in front of their entire region and report their sales progress that week or, if they had no sales, had to pass. She had never experienced anything like this -- the one chance each week to show your peers what you were capable of.

During one roll call, after her very first successful week of selling, Lisa stood up and reported all the sales that she had made that week. It was a significant accomplishment for a new salesperson, let alone a woman, and she was so excited. Later during the meeting, one of the more senior salespeople who doubted her ability approached her and asked, 'You sold something?' as if he didn't believe it. She replied, "Yes, can you believe it?" It was then she started building her confidence but also recognized the importance of building her brand. She worked hard to earn the respect of her peers by consistently exceeding her sales goals and qualifying for multiple Winners Circles at ADP.

So, when she joined SAP, she was ready to continue building her brand. She knew if she didn't bring in qualified deals no one would take her seriously, and she couldn't be successful. Brand building at SAP was more of a necessity. Once she started building success, people wanted to collaborate with her because she was doing well.

Unfortunately, in life (and at work) adversity happens. Lisa has been fortunate for many years in her career not encountering it. But things happen in mysterious ways and at the most inopportune times. Once, when Lisa was positioned for a career promotion, it was derailed suddenly as she had to take unplanned leave from SAP. Her mother had suffered a life-threatening brain aneurysm requiring emergency surgery. For a while, Lisa was not sure her mom would survive, but by the grace of God, prayer was answered, and her mother made a miraculous recovery. When Lisa returned to work, she found she had a new boss who had assumed the position she was targeted for. Realizing she had made the right choice to be with her mom and family, Lisa had no ill-feeling and was just grateful to be back.

Over the next weeks and months, it was clear that this new boss was no gem. He was critical of her success, discounted the work she and her team performed and took credit for her many accomplishments. The harder she tried to please him, the worse he treated her. Lisa was too busy for such nonsense and went on about her business, finally opting to make a lateral career move at SAP. Within three months, the person who had singled her out and caused her so much grief was fired for cause and unprofessional conduct. There is a God, Lisa thought! She has sustained many changes at SAP over the years, and this was just one example of what grace under pressure looks like.

When it comes into play externally, sometimes your brand precedes you, and people may or may not want to collaborate with you because of your reputation. Whatever you do and how you manage a situation, you are going to be judged. Sometimes you make hard decisions, but the way you manage it with discretion, care and compassion is what they will remember.

The brand Lisa continues to demonstrate is four-part, including: 1) the ability to deliver on sales, 2) maintaining client relationships, 3) company loyalty, and 4) technical knowledge. Brand building on SAP was a necessity as well as selling, but Lisa's marketplace brand remains her knowledge of software and her loyal clients along the way.

When asked about her Superpower, Lisa laughed and immediately replied, "My friends tell me I have the 'Italian Mother' syndrome. I care about people and take an interest in their success and letting them know they matter. It's not magic, but just being an authentic human with empathy and humility, recognizing there are lots of ways to be successful and celebrating others when they are." Lisa's Kryptonite is a fear of public speaking which is fed by insecurity. She was concerned about this interview and whether she had anything useful to say. "The good news here is everyone has insecurities," Lisa shared, "but this shouldn't stop you from being remarkably successful. You must feel the fear and do it anyway."

If you are a young person (or even an older one) building or re-building your brand, Lisa counsels the need to practice good judgment and don't do anything you don't want to see in the headlines. Don't plagiarize and do your own work. Have good self-awareness and stay out of social media.

Lisa's Brand Attributes

- ❖ Likeability
- ❖ Adaptability
- ❖ Resiliency
- ❖ Loyalty
- ❖ Integrity

Final Thoughts

When Lisa reflected on her career and her life, she described herself as an average person who has had exceptional opportunities that she has taken advantage of. She doesn't think of herself as unique, but she does think that she has been lucky to have different chances for success. When Lisa commits, she will make it work.

"Sometimes you must take chances," Lisa said, "and if they don't work, you need to move on. Don't be afraid to fail fast because you don't want to have regrets – life is too short. You can't learn if you don't try. Success requires a lot of failures."

Upon meeting Lisa, the last attribute that would come to mind is 'average.' The word 'extraordinary' is better suited to describe her. She has managed to survive in a competitive technology industry for almost three decades. She is not only a powerhouse in the utility industry but also a woman that will go down in the history books at SAP.

Chapter Highlights	Description
Background	Early successful sales at ADP, experienced "roll calls'-built confidence and respect by consistently exceeding sales goals.
Early Aspirations	Be a leader in sales, faced skepticism from peers to build brand and earn respect.
Career Progression	From a single mother to a global leader in the Utilities Industry and SAP for over 28 years.
Superpower	"Italian Mother" syndrome – caring for others and taking an interest in their success, while remaining authentic and humble.
Kryptonite	Fear of public speaking.
Technical Expertise	Solid technical experience in the industry, with the ability to evaluate risks and solutions.
Executive Trust	Balances protecting the team and applying executive pressure to remove impediments.
Industry Recognition	Acknowledged by competition for superior knowledge, leadership, and lasting relationships.

Lisa recently relocated to St. Augustine, FL, with her husband, Mike and their Doberman, Kaiser. Her son, Adam and daughter-in-law, Amanda also reside in Florida, along with other family members.

More information can be found about Lisa at her LinkedIn profile at https://linkedin.com/in/lisadalesandrodichristofer

Chapter 5:
Lakshmi Ravindran
Chief Operating Officer of NCR Solutions

From the Author:

I met Lakshmi in 2012 when we were both partners at IBM. In her tenure there, she was known as a woman that 'got things done.' At one time, she served as the vice president and head of program delivery at a major Northeast utility. I remember thinking: I share the same title as partner with Lakshmi, but I could and would not identify myself in the role she played, even though I have an Information Technology degree from college.

She was also known as a SME in SAP Customer Information Systems. She was often tapped as a thought leader and led selections and implementations of an integral piece of the utility, customer business. The customer business environment is known as the cash register of the utility. A bad implementation costs people jobs and lands the utility on the front pages of local and national newspapers.

Recently, I encountered her again in 2020 on a CIS project in the New England area. Most people, including my firm, didn't know her history, but I did. When I saw that she was the client program director, I sighed with relief. We have been working together side by side for a couple of years now, and I have watched her grow as a professional and as a person.

I recently found out that in 2011 her husband co-founded NCR Solutions, focused on Utilities SAP Customer Relationship & Billing consulting and developed a renewable energy solution for Community Shared Solar / Community-Based Renewable Energy. She serves as chief operating officer. Her journey is one worth sharing and why she is profiled in this book. – C.T.C.

Leadership and Personal Work History

When Lakshmi started the interview for her chapter, her background and international experience came so fast and furious it was hard to comprehend, much less capture.

She was the youngest of four children, born and raised in India. She grew up knowing that education is the key to success in all aspects of life. After high school, she received a Bachelor of Science in Physics and went on to receive a Master of Science in Physics and a Master of Business Administration. She became obsessed with being knowledgeable in all things, especially in computers and received a Post Graduate Diploma in Computer Science and Applications, Human Resource Management and Finance Management. After that extensive education, it became time to find a job, and she was determined to do so using her computer skills. Computer jobs were rare in India at that time, but she was steadfast in pursuing her goal in computers, which was considered going 'off the beaten path.'

Her first job was at a sugar manufacturing company, a division of a large conglomerate. She was instrumental in computerizing their end-to-end manufacturing process, starting with the procurement of raw material (sugar cane) and ending with product, where she designed and developed programs in BASIC and COBOL for several applications. After several years there, she ventured to other companies and then landed at an enterprise resource planning (ERP) company as a solution architect. She was fascinated by the concept of ERP, as it provided a single source of truth across the organization by consolidating siloed systems and processes. She was an associate editor of their in-house technical magazine and was chosen to lead an ERP competitive analysis effort, including SAP, which would eventually prove to be pivotal in Lakshmi's career.

She and her husband were looking for a place to move, where there was less pollution and corruption. They moved to New Zealand in 1997, where she landed a job at a utility consulting firm. There, she began her journey with SAP as a technical project leader.

Her first SAP project was at a utility in Auckland, New Zealand. This utility was chosen by SAP as one of the six in the world to pilot SAP's IS-U/CCS solution, which is now SAP Customer Relationship & Billing (CR&B). At the time, SAP required utility industry knowledge from around the world for the development of their SAP CR&B product. A team of people representing each of the six pilot customers was chosen to participate in a think tank at SAP Labs in Palo Alto, CA, to contribute each of their country's specific utility industry knowledge. Lakshmi was an attendee, interacting with SAP CR&B product development teams from Palo Alto and Waldorf, Germany. She was also one of the key advisors in an SAP CR&B benchmarking team for a hardware sizing tools initiative at a large utility in Europe, with eight million customers in 1998. Large volumes of utility batch jobs were a big challenge for SAP during the initial period. The level of involvement she had is significant because the SAP CR&B product was in its infancy, and she was among the very few who had the opportunity to be there when it all began.

Her career as an SAP/Utilities Industry leader was about to take off. The other SAP pilot customers who participated in the think tank were so impressed with her skill set that a large Northeast utility requested she join their project. Based on just two weeks of engaging her (and seeing her depth of knowledge and strategic thinking), the utility wanted to not only continue her engagement but wanted her to bring a team of more than 25 people from her consulting firm with her. She developed the first 'phased data conversion' and go-live cutover strategy for SAP CR&B for conversion of 2.5 million legacy customers on a live SAP R/3 system. At that time, she was personally associated with three of six SAP CR&B pilot implementations around the world. She was also so well-recognized in the SAP community, so much so that many other large utilities consulted her while evaluating SAP for their CIS replacement or when they had issues during their SAP CR&B implementation.

She progressed to senior leadership roles, from technical project leader to executive vice president and served on the Board of Directors of the company during her 14 years in the consulting firm she started with and continued to grow through acquisitions. After New Zealand, she sold and successfully led various large SAP CR&B implementation projects in multiple countries around the world, too many to name.

She has not only been a client-facing vendor/partner, but she has also worked directly for two major utilities, one in Texas (she went back to the vendor community at IBM as partner in the Global Business Services organization), and the other when IBM seconded her to a client role at a Northeast utility, in the role when we first met.

After leaving IBM in 2017, she stayed true to her passion to pursue the 'next big thing in tech,' as she did at each juncture, like specializing in electronics during her Master of Science in Physics degree, building her career in computers and switching to ERP solutions and SAP as ERP solutions started evolving. Similarly, she was excited when her husband co-founded NCR Solutions and started an initiative in renewable energy. Renewable production of community-shared solar is a game changer product for consumers who cannot place solar at their home or business and allows those customers to benefit from solar generation. Their company found white space in the utility renewable energy market and developed a renewable energy solution for Community Shared Solar (CSS) / Community-Based Renewable Energy (CBRE), which augmented and complemented the Utility CIS solution. Lakshmi joined her husband as chief operating officer at NCR Solutions.

Career Foundation

Her career as a global leader and the opportunities she has been given can never be bought. She has gained insight into some of the premier global companies and learned to form teams on different spectrums, with many types of cultures and customs.

One of her first tasks in her project management role was to form a team - within a few weeks of moving to a new country in a leadership role for a large SAP CR&B project. Since it was her first time recruiting a multi-national team, she knew that the team should be composed of someone who had SAP expertise and experience, someone with strong knowledge of relevant technologies for integrations and someone who was collaborative and could also "protect me from myself." Lakshmi embraced two important criteria:

1. "Attitude OVER Aptitude"

To ensure the three important Cs of teamwork - communication, collaboration and coordination - were achieved, she believed strongly that attitude trumped expertise. Leaders such as Lakshmi build high performing teams. She hired amazing talent that she molded into those teams, put attitude over aptitude, weeded out weak links, provided guidance on improvement and rewarded strength while cutting weakness.

In a project environment, striking the right balance enables individuals to improve performance versus the risk to project delivery. However, she did lean into her mentoring skills and made sure she could provide guidance to those who showed the tenacity to make improvements and show progress.

As a leader, Lakshmi believes it is crucial to assess whether 'can't do' or 'won't do,' is the cause of sub-optimal performance by team members and, in turn, tailor coaching or mentoring accordingly. She believes the leader bears responsibility if it is a 'can't do' and must ensure that proper training and tools are in place to perform the job. The secret, she found, was not to be aggressive but assertive where you need to show two quite different management traits. And she was quick to learn and demonstrate the difference.

2. "Be assertive NOT aggressive!"

She managed teams of varying sizes, starting with small to large teams of 1,000 people. The key, says Lakshmi, has always been to keep the team together. In that way, she learned to be sensitive to other cultures even as she composed the team. Early on, she realized she had the natural ability to keep large project staff motivated and retain them for the duration of the project, even those projects that crossed multiple years. She was blessed with high performing staff members because she had built them by keeping them motivated and optimized once they were in place, quite a challenge.

Like many other tremendously successful women profiled in this book, her mother was her rock growing up. She stood by Lakshmi and gave her the support and opportunity to explore many areas in which to learn. The values Lakshmi stands by today were learned from her mother.

She credits and dedicates the success of her career to her husband, a mentor both personally and professionally. He supported and motivated her through her career journey of over three decades, providing guidance every step of the way and constantly encouraged her to build the skills and capabilities to reach greater heights. She says he enabled her to break the ceiling of her own aspirations to shoot for greater goals in her career. Women in careers such as hers also look to surround themselves with a support system, and it most certainly begins at home.

When it comes to women leaders whom she admires, she recalls India's Prime Minister Indira Gandhi, whose almost 16-year term spanned Lakshmi's childhood through her college days. Seeing Gandhi in power made it seem natural to Lakshmi as a young girl that women can achieve great leadership positions. She says Gandhi's famous quote is something she bears in mind and that every aspiring woman leader must, as well, to reach great heights.

> *"To be liberated, woman must feel free to be herself, not in rivalry to man but the context of her own capacity and her personality."* - **Indira Gandhi**

Along the way, Lakshmi has witnessed many outstanding women leaders within the utility industry that have risen to great leadership positions. She has admiration and respect for the women leaders with whom she has worked and says who she is today is a culmination of the various traits and qualities that she absorbed along the way from these women.

One such woman leader had this to say about her, which Lakshmi believes is a perfect characterization of her leadership style.

> *'Many women professionals in industry, not just in the utility industry, leave their heart and soul aside when they are trying to accomplish their career goals.'*

Lakshmi has been focused on keeping her heart and soul in everything she does. She believes adamantly that if you take care of your team, they will take care of the client, and thus they will deliver.

To that point, she takes care of her team, though not in a formal mentoring program. She has been on projects with hundreds of consultants that have asked for her help, from reading an email to a client to dealing with leadership or peers. She has helped her staff lean in on being more assertive in demonstrating more diplomacy. Based on her international expertise and her skills developed by working with so many cultures, she can give sage as well as stern guidance with grace and without hurting anyone's ego and feelings. That's quite a skillset!

Delivering Exceptional Client Service – Team Development

When delivering exceptional client service, Lakshmi believes it MUST begin with developing a high performing team. While that sounds cliché, even textbook, mutual respect and trust in the relationships when building these teams are key and integral to success. If she is not fortunate to build the team from the beginning of the project, when she takes over she makes sure she knows the names of everyone on the project. She learns something personal about her staff and makes sure she observes and gives compliments to those that are going the extra mile. She works to gain their trust as quickly as she can, as this is essential for development, especially if you are inheriting a team from a prior manager. Everyone on these projects is there because they are intelligent, qualified and diligent. Mutual respect and trust are vital, and human-to-human interactions both personally and professionally make teams stronger.

On large project teams, especially those that are spread across the world, the key to success is to facilitate the staff to be self-motivated and self-disciplined. A saying that became engrained in her from childhood (which she started believing helped her growth as a person later in life) and one she often tells her team is, "Do your duty, don't expect the reward," implying that the rewards will come. Although, initially it seemed counterintuitive, and something 'easier said than done,' she genuinely started believing it and never paused to see who was being rewarded while delivering to clients. Her father-in-law, an inspiration to her, personified this saying in the way he lived and achieved great things as a revered leader and a role model for many. Lakshmi feels this is relevant on projects because any resource who is going the extra mile, working hard in the middle of the night to meet a deadline, yet thinks. 'Who is noticing, and will I be rewarded for this?' should know that every single person is invaluable to the project and their contribution will be noticed and rewarded.

> *"No one feels intimidated by me, so that goes a long way to get people to open up to me, which helps with building trust quickly. I am blessed with that personality trait in running organizations and managing large teams."*
> **- Lakshmi Ravindran**

All along her career, Lakshmi makes the time to form her large staff into smaller groups of 10 or less. She arranges outings, plays games and organizes activities that promote teamwork and fun outside of the project. She also focuses on bringing teams such as Technical and Business (both client and consultants) that don't normally work together on outings, not just her consulting team.

Over many years of consulting and project management, Lakshmi has found that building a successful team is three-fold. It's not just about her consulting staff and the client's but also other consulting firms with the same goal of ensuring that they are successful as a group entity for that client. As an example, one outing might have the theme, 'Talk about anything but work,' to make everyone comfortable and most importantly build trust.

When she looks at new consultants for her projects (both graduates and experienced hires), she looks for their aspirations and temperaments. Even seasoned professionals need to project a good attitude for the tasks ahead, and they need to set a good example for the younger generation that they will be surrounded with, even managing. For entry level consultants, she acknowledges goals that they may have, and she spends time with them initially to assess where they may have potential so she can guide them. For tenured professionals, she needs them to demonstrate organization, people skills and most importantly healthy attitudes. When discord does occur, she demands that they work it out. She reminds them sternly and only once:

> *"Team, I am not blind or deaf to what is going on among you. I need each of you here, so please figure out how to collaborate with each other!"* - **Lakshmi Ravindran**

Once that coaching is received, the issue often resolves itself. If the discord continues, Lakshmi steps in, assesses the problem and acts quickly. There is no room on a project, especially one that is moving swiftly and governed by tight deadlines, budget and milestones, for nonsense. It is managed, the course is corrected, and the plan is re-calibrated and continued.

Of course, as a leader of a team or even a project manager, adversity is part of the game. When Lakshmi was asked about difficulty from other women (and men), she pondered long. When she replied, she answered with two thoughts about the trouble:

1. They don't like me (a woman) in the role because they think I am not qualified to perform.

2. They don't like what I have to say or do.

If it's the first, there is not much she could do about it, and so 'it is what it is.' If it's the second, she would try to work it out in a conversation. If that conversation didn't bring agreement, then she must agree to disagree.

What is interesting about Lakshmi's trials and tribulations with others is that most of those who were initially against her have become friends and brought her in to collaborate on projects they were leading. How is that for turning a negative into a positive!

No one can talk about client service and team development without talking about the potential for failure. Of course, not one of us wants to flounder, but it's paramount that if you do, you get up, dust yourself off and learn how to avoid making the same mistake. When looking at Lakshmi's career, she has been fortunate not to have fallen short frequently and just by meeting her once, you will understand immediately that she has higher standards for herself than she does others. So, it would make sense that she thinks that every project she managed had certain aspects that she felt didn't meet the mark. But she was dedicated to the cause so everyone around her would succeed. That said, not every day is a winning day. With failure, even a small one, comes the opportunity to pause, re-evaluate, return stronger and do better!

Building a Brand

Lakshmi's brand is unique from most profiled in this book. She was born and raised in India, the youngest of four kids raised by strong parents, surrounded by loving and affectionate siblings and family. Her sisters and brother were educated and had other aspirations, but Lakshmi wanted to learn about computers, and she made that her goal from an early age. With the love and support from her mother, she was tenacious and followed her own path on what she wanted to do and achieve. The traits she admired most about her father were his mild manner and how meticulously disciplined he was when executing anything he undertook. She saw how much people loved and trusted him because of those traits. So, as she started to build her brand in her early years, Lakshmi knew she wanted to be known as someone who led with her heart, was assertive and not aggressive, someone who stayed true to her values.

From her early career as a computer programmer in a sugar company in India to one of the global leaders in the utilities industry and SAP that she is today, Lakshmi is someone who has stayed true to her values and delivered expertise to her clients. In doing that, she makes sure she fosters her teams and ensures that they grow and continue to be successful long after the project ends.

Establishing a strong and nurturing relationship with clients and team members is key and essential to every project in building a great brand in the marketplace. Every relationship is a building block on your brand, and at the end of your career, how you have treated people will either bring great joy or great despair.

Early in Lakshmi's career, she learned to drop her guard and be transparent in her communication. She does not pick and choose her words. She is open and honest. In every conversation, she demonstrates that she is trustworthy with no hidden agenda. She separates her role at the client organization from the person, so when she is meeting someone outside of work, she is the person. When she is in a business meeting, she assumes her role. But in both situations, they can trust her to do the right things. She develops those relationships, but it begins as the person and then develops into the role.

> *"Trust is a brand, and great responsibility comes with that trust."* - **Lakshmi Ravindran**

There are so many things Lakshmi has demonstrated that can help professionals start building their brand, things like being knowledgeable and trustworthy, developing teams that deliver exceptional client value and instilling confidence in her clients that their project will be on time and on budget, especially with a project such as SAP that demands knowledge of the product and the industry.

She keeps herself current in all aspects of the industry and SAP to deliver value. Many agree Lakshmi's best Superpower is her unique talent in interacting with all types of people, regardless of race or culture. With her international expertise and calm demeanor, her grace under pressure and knowledge of the human psyche, she has incredible people skills. Since she appears benign, she intimidates few. This demeanor serves her well, and she speaks to all people as she would a friend.

However, that Superpower can quickly become her Kryptonite. She is considerate, which can easily be taken advantage of. While her consideration might look like weakness, one can rest assured that she is always looking for the good—both in people and situations. In this way, leading with her heart doesn't mean her head isn't far behind. Demonstrating knowledge through the heart isn't at all a sign of weakness; it's one of strength and is immediately disarming. And accomplishing client projects without drama or anger but instead with tremendous success, on-time and on-budget is a brand any project director would embrace at the end of a long and fruitful career.

While composing this chapter, a few quotes were discovered that further define Lakshmi's brand:

Quotes from Her Clients:

- 'I value your wise counsel and leadership.'

- 'You are a strong and talented woman.'

- 'I sleep better knowing you are on watch.'

- 'Coaching and mentoring teams is your strength, making you an ideal leader for complex projects with large teams and building practices.'

- 'Your contribution and leadership are making a remarkable difference to our users and our customers.'

- 'Thank you, Lakshmi, for your brilliant leadership and counsel. Without your expertise and diplomatic problem-solving abilities, our success to date would not have been remotely possible. We are lucky to have you!'

- 'Leadership of large implementations such as CIS programs requires someone who can adeptly straddle many universes and maintain grace under pressure. I have watched Lakshmi operate in this manner for years, and she has been a great mentor for me as a woman in tech, as well as many others she has led.'

- 'Lakshmi has been a fabulous partner in our CIS implementation, and I have learned much from her.'

- 'Like Lakshmi said, 'We are going to add hardware to solve an issue.'' (The chief information officer went against the recommendation of his senior leadership team and leaders of three big consulting firms and adopted Lakshmi's advice.)

Her success is fueled by several attributes which I believe are the ingredients for success:

- First, she has solid technical experience to draw on when teams need to make decisions and recommend a logical solution. She can ferret out things that are risky, evaluate the level of effort quickly and prevent things from going too far down the wrong track.

- Second, for programs of this magnitude, you need a leader who can build and maintain executive trust and yet be transparent when there are issues. She knows how to balance the need to protect the team versus applying executive pressure to remove impediments.

- Last, Lakshmi is adept at helping resolve conflicts that invariably arise when teams comprised of several parties get together to do something hard. I've watched her listen to teams and navigate them through conflicts to get to quick resolutions. It doesn't matter if it's an individual developer on a team or a leader in a particular business unit, she is able to leverage her experience to provide advice or drive a conclusion.

Quotes from Her Competition:

- 'Lakshmi, you are pulling the rug out from under my feet with the trust and respect you have gained from this client. Instead of the company winning more projects, they were losing, due to Lakshmi's demonstration of superior knowledge and leadership. She has deep industry expertise, delivers results and develops strong nurturing relationships that last a lifetime!'

Lakshmi's Brand Attributes

- ❖ Transparency
- ❖ Trustworthiness
- ❖ Technical Prowess
- ❖ Meditation Skills
- ❖ Quiet Elegance

Final Thoughts

Lakshmi has had the privilege of collaborating with many women in the utility industry since leaving the sugar company back in India. However, all the advice she gives (in fact, this applies to all the women profiled in this book) is applicable to both women (and men) across all industries. She has been fortunate to give many women well-deserved opportunities and has been able to coach and mentor them too.

When asked what she wants her legacy to be after a long, fruitful career, she was quick to respond:

- Someone that used the opportunities she was blessed to receive.

- Someone that helped others reach their highest potential.

- Someone that delivered high value projects in the industry.

- Someone that could bridge the gap between technology and people skills.

She really hopes that she has given words of support and encouragement, not just "lip service." She wants each person to make everyday count and ensure they work with their heart, not just their head. She also wants everyone to remember that she always valued her team and hopes that they value each other.

Someone once told her: 'People think your ways of working are seen as a weakness, but we think it's a strength. We have learned from that and emulate that as we lead our team every day.'

She added one final thought as we finished our conversation:

> *"Learn everything you can. Bring in humility when you're wrong. Never hesitate to go the extra mile. Being a manager is about you, but being a leader is about your team. Mentor the team to achieve, enjoy the benefit of that and know that when you leave, they will be better than when you were there!"* **- Lakshmi Ravindran**

Chapter Highlights	Description
Background	Born and raised in India, inspired by strong family values and discipline.
Early Aspirations	Interest in computers from a young age, with tenacity to pursue her goals.
Value-Driven Leadership	Known for leading with her heart, being assertive without aggression and staying true to values.
Career Progression	From a computer programmer to a global leader in the utilities industry and SAP.
Relationship Building	Fosters strong relationships with clients and team members, ensuring their growth.
Communication Style	Transparent, open and honest, earning trust with no hidden agenda.
Superpower	Unique talent in interacting with people of all races and cultures, with international expertise.
Kryptonite	Considerate nature that could be taken advantage of but also seen as a strength.
Technical Expertise	Solid technical experience in the industry, with the ability to evaluate risks and solutions.
Executive Trust	Balances protecting the team and applying executive pressure to remove impediments.
Conflict Resolution	Skilled at navigating teams through conflicts to reach quick resolutions.

Client Testimonials	Praised for wise counsel, leadership, mentoring and successful project management.
Industry Recognition	Acknowledged by competition for superior knowledge, leadership and lasting relationships.

Lakshmi lives with her husband in Irving, TX, and enjoys cooking and entertaining in her beautiful home. More information can be found about her on LinkedIn at https://www.linkedin.com/in/lakshmi-ravindran-6905b57/

Chapter 6:
Maureen Coveney Bolen
Chief Revenue Officer - delaware North America

F rom the Author:

When I was reviewing my list of women to profile, IUCX (formerly CS Week) CEO Rod Litke suggested I profile Maureen, and I loved the idea. I have observed Maureen Bolen for many years, both in the utility market at conferences, as a competitor and now as a friend. She has always been well respected in my social and working circles, and when we've met, she has always had a smile on her face. I knew she was a special lady, but I had no idea how extraordinary until I spent time interviewing her for this chapter.

Her background and her journey to the industry as a client-facing partner is extremely unique, as you will soon learn.

Her passion for her work, clients and employees is shown clearly in Maureen's stories. I am extremely proud of having profiled her and hope you will enjoy reading her story as much as I enjoyed writing it. - C.T.C.

Leadership and Personal Work History

From the first time you meet Maureen, you can tell she is a highly intellectual person. Her pedigree started in 1992 with an undergraduate degree in mechanical and nuclear engineering from the University of California, Berkeley. She received a master's degree in nuclear engineering in 1997, again from Berkeley, in nine months, all while working full-time.

She began her career as a mechanical and nuclear engineer at GE Nuclear Energy (GENE). She intended to pursue a PhD in thermal hydraulics; however, she met friends that were enrolled in one of her senior nuclear engineering courses from GENE. They persuaded her to interview, she got the offer, and her journey began.

GE believed in taking entry level persons and pouring technical and leadership training into them, while allowing them to transition through rotations. Maureen was there for almost five years and performed seven roles during that time, all with different areas of engineering focus. GE taught soft skills such as project and time management, Six Sigma and Myers-Briggs. GE also encouraged its new engineers to accrue a diversity of experience, so she worked on advanced reactor design, information technology and field engineering projects, including a remotely operated vehicle deployed in Japan. Additionally, GENE senior engineers taught the student to learn engineering fundamentals, and in her case, it was all with GE's Boiling Water Reactor fleet. After a course, they were split into groups and assigned a (real) GE problem set that would require the application of those fundamentals. Teams were usually given one week to solve the problem and report out. These exercises taught young engineers how to collaborate, divide and conquer, articulate and present a solution, as well as grade peers.

The teams usually worked 60 or more hours a week to perform rotational assignments, in addition to normal course work. No one spoke of 'work-life balance.' Instead, leaders communicated that 'casual overtime' and 'face time' was a necessary thing to advance your career. It wasn't optional.

As an additional benefit, GE offered the entire team their master's degrees if they could complete the program in nine months. And Maureen accepted that challenge, got her masters, all while continuing her work at GE.

Maureen married just before the start of her master's program, and at the completion of that program, she left GE when she and her husband decided to relocate to Southern California where they could balance dual careers. After moving, she became a consultant for Science Applications International Corporation (SAIC), a government military contractor that provides technical, engineering and information technology services to the US government.

Her first assignment was at San Onofre Nuclear Generating Station (SONGS) to lead a program that would allow SONGS to relax certain critical component testing intervals upon the US Nuclear Regulatory Commission's (NRC) approval. She led the team, organized the information (creating her first Access database), wrote the regulatory submittal and received NRC approval for SCE to implement the program. It was the second approval of its kind in the industry. She was assigned additional work in testing and training for a suite of SAIC Plant Operations software. Within two years, she was promoted to Product Management and then on to Group Management.

During her nuclear tenure at SAIC, Maureen met J. Patrick (Pat) Kennedy, Founder and CEO of the company, OSIsoft, the maker of a real-time data management platform called the PI System. After several years as the group manager at SAIC, and accomplishing the NRC approval, Maureen's desire to take on new challenges bubbled up. Always curious and a lifelong learner, Maureen was intrigued when Mr. Kennedy approached her to join his company.

She joined OSIsoft in 2004 to lead Marketing, an area of the business for which she had not yet been responsible. In just a few years and much success within this newly proven talent, she established the Product Management division (OSIsoft has since been acquired by AVEVA). She was clearly demonstrating a brand that was not only technical but also personable.

At OSIsoft, Maureen established an approach to prioritizing industry requests and led annual conferences. Her team focused on providing educational content and enabling customers – from power generation, oil and gas, chemicals, pulp and paper, and other industries – to share their stories and lessons learned.

There, she was introduced to the software giant, SAP. As she heard more about the company, she felt she could combine her love of consulting, her knowledge of utilities and her technical acumen to excel at OSIsoft. After several rewarding years, she decided to leave OSIsoft and take her career in yet another direction.

Several of her colleagues were at SAP, so she joined the company in 2007 where again her focus was on utilities. As an industry principal, Maureen worked with large and small utilities to plan their SAP technology adoption roadmaps and worked with SAP to prioritize requirements in the solutions portfolio.

Henry Bailey, her manager, recognized the value of her connecting SAP software users together to share best practices. He tapped Maureen to launch SAP North America (NA) – a utilities-focused conference. Even though she had no budget, Maureen excelled and received much interest before it started. In 2008, she launched the SAP for Utilities NA Conference and ran that program with a company called Eventure for three years. It was so successful, SAP realized that they should be hosting this event and then brought it back to their SAP utilities division. It has been rebranded SAP4U and is one of the most highly anticipated conferences of the year for utilities and partner vendors.

While at SAP, Southern California Edison's (SCE) chief information officer called her to join the utility as a director of IT. Maureen had met Mahvash Yazdi earlier in her career, and he had become a personal mentor as her career progressed. She knew she had to help where she could. So, she spoke to the leadership at SAP and made the decision to leave as benefits would be realized by both SCE and SAP. She began her journey with SCE in April 2010.

Her new job would be to help stabilize the SAP portfolio, specifically for power (nuclear) generation which had struggled with the change from its many home-grown applications. Leading that charge, she corrected process operations within 18 months in both the SAP and non-SAP footprint. Helping out her old friend had major implications; she was now known as a recognized expert in SAP Utilities software implementations and triage.

In addition to her engineering background, while at SCE she became certified in a specific leadership methodology called Facilitative Leadership. FL is a way to effect change as a leader, and it works at every level of leadership. If we seek to make a change, the FL methodology helps us to define the change in terms of a 'Big Picture' - Where are we now? Where are we headed? - and then involve key stakeholders to help create the vision, identify the impediments to realizing the Big Picture and solve them so that those impediments can be addressed effectively. This leadership program also helped her continue to build her brand.

During her tenure, the power generation operation began to demonstrate marked improvement in process efficiency, effectiveness and organizational alignment. She then joined the SCE Business Transformation team as a director of leadership and organizational effectiveness. Her job was to train all leaders from supervisors through the VP and C-level to be 'facilitative leaders' who guide stakeholders through the change journey, leaving no key stakeholder behind. However, in June 2013, SCE decided to decommission the SONGS program, which led her to consider a role outside the utility, one in consulting. After several years working with other companies, she began her own company in 2015, the Bolen Group.

Now enlightened by what utilities really needed in its consultants and in its solutions, she returned to what would make it easier to accept and lead change. These solutions turned out to be focused back to SAP because she honestly believed (and still believes) that the SAP platform offers so many possibilities.

In 2019, she started collaborating with a company that she knew well: Utegration. Prior employees of SAP formed the company. While collaborating with them, she was recruited and then hired by Utegration to serve as its chief growth officer, working beside friends and mentors CEO Bart Thielbar, Chief Strategy Officer Henry Bailey, Chief Solutioning Officer Gary Hayes and Director of Marketing Pam Jeffries. Utegration later agreed to let her lead the development of a pre-configured content solution for SAP S/4HANA (Utility4U™), a well-known product used in the industry today.

In December 2022, Utegration was acquired by Cognizant, and Maureen led the SAP practice focused on Manufacturing, Logistics, Energy and Utilities (MLEU), which allows her to convert offerings and approaches across not just energy and utilities, but other adjacent industries. In mid-2024, she was solicited and hired by a new firm to help enhance their market presence in the SAP community in North America, Delaware NA. A position she enjoys today.

Maureen's career and leadership journey, culminating as an industry expert in utility software, was unconventional and grounded in her love for engineering and technical challenges. Maureen has a gift and love for the study of transfer thermal dynamics. Sharing her story is a reminder that being technically brilliant does not make you socially awkward. Maureen is truly a very well-rounded individual!

Career Foundation

Maureen's career foundation has been built on a humble background. Upon meeting her, that humility shines. She's from a blue-collar family. Her father was an auto mechanic; her mother, a food service worker who eventually became the first female maintenance lead for her school district, Santa Rosa City Schools.

She loved learning, especially math, English, history and music. Her personal hero was her maternal grandfather, and she was remarkably close to him. He was a teacher, a coach and a college advisor. He cared deeply about his community of young, impressionable minds, and according to Maureen, he made an impact on the lives he mentored.

She strived to learn as much as she could and was the top student in a class of 579 graduates. She earned her place in Berkeley, the only place she sought to go to college.

However, just before she was due to leave for college, her parents separated which caused a different plan to emerge. She remained committed to attending, but it turned out, even with a few scholarships, it wasn't enough. She found a job in a local healthcare business, making it possible to earn a living and pay for college by working usually 28 to 32 hours a week, all while attending engineering classes at Berkeley. Those were grueling, tough years. Engineering is a discipline unto itself, and it demands time.

While trying to manage all of this, she lost her father to lung cancer when she was only 19 years old and simultaneously watched her brother (and best friend) become a drug addict. She struggled to balance grief with the task at hand.

She persisted with the emotional support of her mother, her girlfriends and family who repeatedly said, "You can do this, Moe."

> *"And as soon as I believed I could do it, I did!"*
> **– Maureen Coveney Bolen**

She found she loved everything about engineering—heat transfer, thermal dynamics, statistics and dynamics, mechanical design, partial differential equations. Her career foundation is different than most. When meeting her, she is kind and jovial, full of fun and vigor, and one would never know her background and upbringing. Sharing her story is a reminder that while you may never know where a person is from or what obstacles they've overcome, success is a matter of mind and resiliency. Maureen is living proof!

Delivering Exceptional Client Service – Team Development

Maureen's teams think of her as being committed to their success and to their customers' success. Her mantra is to create a client-driven organization both internally and externally. A leader must seek to understand what comprises success and remain engaged throughout program delivery by creating a team, then establishing how each person will be accountable to other members of the team. Once that's complete, it's coaching the best performance out of everyone.

She believes that teams that leverage one another's strengths usually perform the best, and they tend to enjoy the camaraderie that invariably results along the way.

Early on, she read *The Five Dysfunctions of a Team: A Leadership Fable* by Patrick M. Lencioni, and she now encourages her team to read it as well. She asks the team to read this book as a part of their on-boarding to her team. The shared experience of reading and discussing this book allows the teams to 'fast forward' their ability to leverage each other's strengths. To establish trust, she defines her team's purpose and encourages everyone to work together to be individually accountable to each other to achieve the desired outcome.

Maureen believes the industry wants and needs formal and informal strategic advisors (more so than they did in the past). She regularly encourages her staff to build their experience base, so they can become trusted advisors for the clients they serve. She enjoys watching teams grow into chief information officers, counselors and collaborators, and this brings both the clients and team members a great deal of personal satisfaction.

She inspires and engages by getting to know team members on an individual basis and by taking an interest in their work. She does that in the way that works best for each team and individual. Leadership engagement – active involvement – keeps people motivated to create a deliverable that will be the best it can be. For example, when teams are working on an oral presentation, she listens to each person's delivery to help them articulate their key messages and to practice answering customer questions. This helps them develop 'game day' confidence for the actual oral event.

People tell Maureen that her best leadership attribute is that she is genuine, and her experience is diverse, both professionally and personally. She can relate to anyone and likes to put those she meets and interacts with at ease and develop rapport, so they are free to answer her questions. By creating a safe space for her staff and clients, Maureen feels she can make workplace situations better, and thus work together to resolve any issues they may be facing.

When she looks for new consultants to hire for her practice, she looks for the following attributes:

- ○ **Customer service**. She finds that people who have performed customer service roles – for example, someone who worked at an In-and-Out Burger during high school or college — tend to be client-driven.

- ○ **Initiative**. GE trained her to look for people who have this quality. Paired with self-confidence, initiative tends to lead to better individual performance and often to better team performance and innovation (even through trial and error). She prefers collaborating with people who take the initiative to pursue an opportunity, then see it through to the end.

When asked about working with adversity, she feels fortunate to be able to share that she has felt supported by both women and men throughout her career, from peers to leaders to industry colleagues. Have there been times when she hasn't agreed with a specific approach or strategy? Sure; she thinks that's natural. But it's her upbringing (she was surrounded by strong-willed family members and equally strong-willed best friends at different points in her life that allows Maureen to see debate as a natural occurrence and one that she anticipates and enjoys because conflict will reveal the best answer for a given set of circumstances.

Of course, there have been pivotal, crucial career moments where she learned something about herself that became ingrained in how she views herself today. During the mid-'90s, for example, she was assigned to a field engineering project in which the project manager hired a contractor with a specific skill set and made him lead on the project. The contractor was quite gifted; however, he was openly derisive and insulting toward the younger GE engineers on the program, including Maureen. She raised her concerns about this contractor's behavior to the PM and to program leadership. The PM said, "You are not as important to the success of this project as that guy is, so you'll just have to deal with it." Program leadership offered to move her to another project. Neither response seemed like the right answer, and both were disappointing. She stayed with the program, seeing it through to the end. She loved what they were able to accomplish together despite negative interactions with the contractor.

She learned much from that situation - namely, quite a bit about engaged leadership and what happens in its absence. When employees raise a behavioral issue to a program leader or to the organization, it's the manager's job to help the employee address the challenge. That contractor deserved an engaged leader to hold him accountable to the rest of the team and to teach him how to treat the team with respect, so the team could perform at its best.

Building a Brand

Maureen started her career in the late '90s when building a brand was not a part of a career plan. However, from the start she saw herself as a strategic advisor to her customers. Maureen learned early on that she could readily relate to their issues and concerns, and by invoking her inner engineer she looked for solutions that would address their problems. She establishes and nurtures strong relationships with clients and employees by reaching out often and even when she doesn't need anything; she just checks in.

Building a brand also leverages continuous feedback, and learning every day helps contribute to how she wants to be seen as a professional. Incorporating learning gained from both clients and her staff and superiors and bringing it into the team to improve them makes living the mantra 'continuous improvement' an active, engaged process. Sharing feedback and then working together to address the bad and enhance the good feedback can be the most satisfying work possible. Human beings have an innate drive to want to do better than they did the last time, so tapping into that drive is essential for continuing to evolve solutions that deliver value.

Maureen considers her Superpower to be her memory, but she also thinks that studying engineering forced a certain problem-solving approach that she leverages every day. She can 'organize chaos,' which she is fond of doing.

Maureen considers her Kryptonite to be chaos. She does not like to 'cycle' people - team members, clients, family. "If we are going to do something, let's do it as close to right as we can, the first time," and she thinks that extends to the creative process. When giving advice to young people on building their brand, Maureen counsels,

"Just jump in; the water's fine!" Just get started, and the act of beginning this journey helps one to identify things that make us enthusiastic. Passion drives personal brand.

Even though there was not brand awareness when she started her career, there were certainly role models, and Maureen attributes the success of her brand to her mother. Maureen emulated her mother, Maggie O'Keefe, who was kind and patient, yet ruthlessly efficient and effective in managing their household. She balanced this by being firm, yet approachable, and she was always available to her brothers and sisters.

Her mother forged a path for herself by becoming the first female maintenance supervisor for the Santa Rosa City School District, where she was both admired and maligned: admired by most because she led with grace and engaged with all to ensure her hometown's schools were in the best shape they could be for the kids who were educated in their buildings and maligned by a few because she was not a man, and maintenance was considered a man's purview. She served as a beacon for Maureen and many young ladies of that generation.

Maureen's Brand Attributes

- ❖ Curious
- ❖ Continuous self-improvement
- ❖ Passionate
- ❖ Strategic Thinker
- ❖ Pioneering Spirit

Final Thoughts

When Maureen reflects on her legacy, she hopes that she has made great contributions to the Power and Utilities sector. She's had many young people seek her out as a mentor across a multitude of industries which has been a wonderful, bi-directional experience.

In the industry, she trusts that all the young people with whom she's served saw her as an approachable, engaged leader who sought to understand and help resolve the issues they faced.

On a personal level, she wants the teams she's built and the solutions she's put in place to survive the test of time. She hopes her team members feel empowered to drive change and to serve as true industry advisors to their clients. And she hopes the solutions they've crafted together will continue to evolve to serve the industry.

She wants her clients to remember her as responsible. She speaks her truth, but she tries to balance it with caring and insights derived from 'walking in their shoes.'

Maureen has three lessons for both men and women:

1. **Relate**. Get to know the people you are serving.

2. **Be authentic**. Make sure you show up with no false pretenses or ulterior motives.

3. **Don't give up**. Sometimes you'll hear the word 'no.' Take it as a starter, go back to the drawing board, hone the solution and the message, and take it back out there.

Chapter Highlights	Description
Career Start	Began in the late '90s without an initial focus on building a brand.
Professional Identity	Views herself as a strategic advisor, relating to customer issues and finding solutions.
Relationship Building	Establishes and nurtures relationships by reaching out often, even without needing anything.
Continuous Improvement	Embraces feedback and learning to enhance professional image and team performance.

Superpower	Exceptional memory and an engineering-driven, problem-solving approach to organize chaos.
Kryptonite	Dislikes chaos and cycling through people, preferring to get things right the first time.
Advice to Others	Encourages jumping in and starting the journey to discover passion and drive personal brand.
Role Model Influence	Inspired by her mother, Maggie O'Keefe, who was kind, patient, efficient and a pioneering leader.
Mother's Legacy	First female maintenance supervisor, leading with grace and engaging with the community.
Personal Values	Balances being firm and approachable, with a focus on availability and support for her team.

Maureen lives with her husband, John Bolen, in Truckee, CA. Together, they have a daughter, Colleen Coveney and a son, Brian Coveney, and three stepchildren, Andrea Richard, Matt Bolen and Jake Bolen. In 2023, Maureen and John adopted a beloved Rottweiler, Dembe, named for a character in the tv series, *The Blacklist*. She is a cooking enthusiast, a lover of game night with family and friends and actively seeks the outdoors whenever her schedule allows. She (still) dreams of being the bass player in a rock 'n roll band. Look to see her playing at Truckee Thursdays in the not-so-distant future!

More information can be found about Maureen on LinkedIn at: https://www.linkedin.com/in/maureen-bolen-6a525a5/

Chapter 7:
Susan Lynch
Managing Director at Accenture

From the Author:

I met Susan Lynch in January 2000 at KPMG. Susan met my plane at Miami International, and instead of dropping off our belongings we proceeded directly to dinner with my new KPMG colleagues for our first meeting. While we were at dinner, the back window of Susan's SUV was shattered, our clothes and briefcases stolen.

After a long interview with Miami's finest detectives, we were told that they would investigate the matter. We arrived at the JW Marriott with a quickly purchased bag of CVS makeup and facial wipes.

Being robbed is devastating and a tremendous invasion of privacy. It was that day that I made a lifetime friend and someone from whom I seek counsel to this day. It is because of her professionalism and grace, as well as deep industry knowledge, that she is a valued member of the utility vendor community. She is an expert in her field, a role model for all the people in her industry (not just women). I watched her evolve at KPMG, rebranded BearingPoint, then PwC, and now Susan is one of my fiercest competitors at Accenture. It is because of her trials and victories that she is profiled in this book. - C.T.C.

Leadership and Personal Work History

Susan Lynch went to the University of Central Florida in the late 1990s and graduated with an undergraduate degree in education.

She had no idea what she wanted to do with her life, so she started her first job as a computer operator and attained her master's degree in information systems design while attending night school.

Afterwards, she started a job with KPMG in 1998. At that time, KPMG was known as one of the elite Big 8 accounting firms and landing a job with them was extremely prestigious, especially as a woman right out of school. She lived in Chicago, and she was told that travel out of such a hub would be easy. She was unsure of what to expect, but the pay was good, and the idea of travel and expense accounts sounded exciting and rewarding.

On her second day, she was given a plane ticket to Grand Rapids, MI. Her first assignment was to assist in writing accounting procedures for a major client. Considering her degrees were in education and instructional systems design, authoring and designing accounting procedures was out of her comfort zone. It was that initial experience and all the uncertainty of what each day would bring as a consultant which kept her rewarded.

After a successful project there, she was assigned to the Mississippi Department of Transportation as a business analyst, collaborating with employees who had built their entire careers in information technology. With that project under her belt, Susan felt determined to push her career forward and take on other challenges.

Soon after working with the state agency, she was assigned to another project, NASA. Being assigned to NASA was both a blessing and a curse. Her first project at NASA was as a senior consultant (she quickly progressed from staff consultant to senior consultant), and she was tasked with installing and implementing a financial and procurement system. Her friendly demeanor and her quick grasp of the assignment made her a hit with the staff. KPMG leadership assigned her to be the data conversion lead, managing a team that had never performed these tasks together. Things were about to get tough.

Working until 3 a.m., travelling five days a week and constantly being on her feet and on point as a leader was exhausting. She continued to work outside her comfort zone, being challenged by many colleagues who were twice her age. She pushed, determined to progress in her career with her sights set on becoming a partner. Being a partner is a coveted position in a Big 8 accounting firm and usually takes many years and tremendous personal sacrifices to rise from a consultant to such an elite position.

In the late 1990s and early 2000s, consulting was a male-dominated industry, especially in the Big 8 accounting firms. However, Susan continued to flourish and get promoted through the ranks to manager. In 2000, we met at KPMG and worked together at a major municipality implementing SPL Worldgroup customer information system (CIS) software. KPMG became successful in that project, and Susan and her team sold CIS implementations across Florida, including Miami-Dade Water and Sewer, City of West Palm Beach and City of Tallahassee, among others.

Her next project was at Jacksonville Electric Authority (JEA), and she commuted to Jacksonville, FL, five days a week, leaving every Monday at 6 a.m. and returning home Friday afternoons. The travel was grueling, but she had been given the tremendous responsibility by management of being the testing lead. She knew that no was not an option, and if she wanted the promotions and the titles, she had to put in the work. There was no short cut to making partner; you worked from the ground up.

While at JEA, KPMG became BearingPoint, the public entity. That shift from a partnership to a corporation changed the game for a lot of young professionals with career goals of becoming partner at KPMG. Around the same time, she became pregnant with her first child. The pregnancy progressed, she took her parental leave and returned to the company part-time. Working part-time in consulting means you work the same amount of time, for half the pay. She felt she was not enough in either area, neither being a parent nor delivering projects. She returned full-time, juggling a demanding consulting job with equally demanding parental responsibilities.

Unfortunately, BearingPoint filed Chapter 11, and that utilities team was purchased by PwC. Susan found herself back on a partnership path and started the promotional journey again. As with all her projects, she under-promised and over-delivered. She became extremely valuable to PwC in both a sales and delivery role, performing above her position title. She was there for 15 years, and as time progressed projects became larger and more complex as utilities became bigger, merged and more multi-dimensional. Utility projects continued to be exciting, but she wanted more.

In 2021, she was approached by Accenture with a proposal like, 'You can define your dream job, and we can help you realize it.' She finally knew exactly what she wanted after 25 years of consulting. She wanted both! That meant a sales and delivery team, expanding her brand and developing exceptional consultants.

Career Foundation

Susan built her career on two things: honesty and integrity. Her mantra to her staff was and still is the same, "Do what you say and say what you're going to do." Her progression over the years speaks volumes, but make no mistake, it was one step at a time. Early in her career, she felt that if she kept her head down, promotions would come naturally. Over the years she learned otherwise. As a woman, she needed to self-promote, a skill not easily acquired.

Building a foundation is also dependent on the people with whom you surround yourself. Being a consultant exposes you to many types of personalities, both within your organization and your clients'. Internally, she has worked under many leadership styles. That exposure, good or bad, shapes the kind of leader you want to become. Some of her toughest managers instilled lessons such as demand excellence and a passion for excellent client service.

One such leader is Charlie Johnson, a retired partner from BearingPoint and later Microsoft. He insisted that every interaction with a client would build a foundation for a trusted advisor position, and eventually that posture would lead to business. He instilled this value in all his consultants, and to this day he is remembered for helping people be their most authentic self.

Other leaders tend to push clients out of their comfort zone and drive them towards innovation. Some lead by connecting and emphasizing teamwork. Susan learned from all her leaders that people want integrity and authenticity. They want to know you care not just about the work but about their individual success.

Over the years, Susan has had to learn communication skills that drive behavior. This, in turn, has allowed for tough conversations that advance self-promotion. That life skill didn't come early in her career. It was after 10 or 15 years in one firm that she realized an epiphany - she was limited in her upward mobility because she was too valuable in her current role. The void she would have left had she been promoted would have been too tough to fill. And leadership would or could not manage that with the client. She didn't allow for self-promotion on this journey, and unfortunately she didn't get promoted.

Now, she equates her reviews – both with her staff and her managers – to a football game. She gives and expects real-time feedback. People, including herself, need feedback on their performance. The basics hold true, not only now but 25 years ago. "Do you share a common vision of success within your role or your project? Are you a good communicator, and do you show up every day?"

In her current position with Accenture, she is a leader, a mentor and a valued member of the executive leadership team. The example set by her current female manager, Samia Tarraf, conveys a vastly different tone – career progression is important, but everyone wants and needs to be valued and recognized for their contributions. Not everyone strives for advancement. Sometimes the best part of the job is when someone says thank you, and Susan aspires to learn from Samia every day. Susan's career started many years ago, but every day leads to someone or something that can continue to make her foundation stronger.

> *"Do what you say and say what you're going to do."*
> **– Susan Lynch**

Delivering Exceptional Client Service through Team Development

Susan is known in the industry as a mentor and developer of extraordinary talent. Many of the young consultants she has coached over the years have moved on to other consulting firms, and occasionally she finds herself competing with them on a project.

No one is prouder to see a past consultant in the client's lobby where she and her team are waiting for oral presentations for a big project. She knows the values she instilled and quietly celebrates the accomplishments they are enjoying.

Learning how to communicate effectively is key to success in Susan's playbook, regardless of her audience's gender. However, women must learn to communicate differently than men. Studies have shown that women need to constantly remind themselves of that, especially when they are with a team of men and women colleagues. Susan suggests setting reminders on their calendars for self-reflection and asking questions, such as:

- Do I have goals and priorities?

- Am I doing it to check a box?

- Who do I want to be?

- Am I the person I thought I would be?

- Do I want to be known as someone that remembers clients' birthdays?

- Do I want to just show up or do I want to be effective today?

When Susan is giving reviews, she begins with, "Are you showing your best and highest value to brand and this firm?" She counsels, "Be intentional," and "Keep your network and brand in the front of your mind."

Developing your storytelling skills is key and integral to developing exceptional client service. It is important to your team, as well as your client, to be able to translate a complex project into an easy to digest dialogue that captures attention and elicits a positive action.

Susan demands that professionalism be paramount, demonstrating those skills and demeanor in person, as well as virtually. In today's omni-channel world, looking people in the eye and being present in the conversation is not always exercised, both with internal management and clients. For in-person meetings, make sure you connect personally with every client leader. Online, be visible, show your face, engage in the conversation. Follow-up calls and in-person meetings with emails that 'stick the landing' are essential; for example: "I enjoyed the meeting today and look forward to providing these action items you requested."

Susan is responsible for a large team in her current role as managing director. When she is hiring or even transferring talent from one internal group to hers, she looks for these skills:

- Can the candidate speak well?

- What is their presence on teams?

- How do they problem solve?

- How do they manage adversity?

- What are their ethical standards?

Not all interactions with teammates and clients are positive. You may get into an uncomfortable position. Part of her team selection is what Susan calls the "It" factor, that intangible grit and perseverance that lets her know that she and the firm can trust you when things are tough.

Good people usually know good people, and a lot of her team are references from her current and past relationships. Because those relationships are built over a career, Susan's loyalty is to her people.

Good leaders are both men and women. There is a cliché that men are easier to work for than women, and that may be true because women assume that they need to work much harder (and they do). As her career has progressed, she feels less need to apologize. She follows her inner voice, feels confident expressing her opinions and if people don't agree, that's okay. She has developed confidence that she'll land on her feet. She bets on herself and seldom loses. Of course, that comes with experience. Seldom do people have that belief in their younger selves.

Susan has had lessons learned as a leader. For example, though she was new to a company, she had joined with a reputation of being able to get complex projects done and done well which yielded new assignments of increasing responsibilities. She quickly found herself on an exceptionally large client project in addition to three other internal projects, all of which required considerable time. As such, she never felt like she showed up at her best at any of them. Knowing that you're spread so thin that nothing looks good is not a pleasant position. Thankfully, her team recognized this dilemma and helped her course correct. Quality versus quantity always wins, and Susan recognizing she had the power to say, "No," made quality paramount.

Building a Brand

Historically, the utilities industry has been characterized by a lack of gender diversity. Men have dominated roles in sectors such as energy, water and telecommunications. Stereotypes and biases have functioned as barriers to women who sought to enter or excel in sales within this sector. To that point, building a strong business brand is an essential component of success in today's competitive marketplace, especially in the vendor space.

When Susan began her career in the '90s, building a brand wasn't considered part of her career path. It wasn't considered a part of anyone's career plan, let alone a woman. Now, she realizes that your brand is not just a logo or a tagline; it's the emotional connection you and your business create with your clients. A powerful business brand can set you apart from your competitors, drive client loyalty, inspire admiration from your colleagues and contribute to long-term success.

When asked how she built her brand, Susan said, "I just showed up." Since this concept was introduced a few short years ago, she has tried to be more intentional. Considering her keys to success and her shortcomings that she has since overcome, Susan identified her Superpower and her Kryptonite.

Susan's Superpower has always been her exceptional good energy. It's a fact that she's been told her entire life, and she often wondered what it meant. It clearly translates to how she makes others feel. That good energy has shaped which people gravitate toward her and the people that want to work on her team. 'Like attracts like,' and she believes that her attitude and positive demeanor has attracted and retained many great consultants throughout the years.

Comparable to other women working in the utility world, Susan is often plagued with 'ultimate imposter syndrome.' That's her Kryptonite. She sometimes feels she shouldn't be sitting at the conference room table, and sometimes her confidence grows shaky. Often women face challenges about their own self-worth and experience inner doubts. Should I be here? Can I contribute? Susan confides that she needs to exercise that muscle that stops herself from negative talk. She becomes very intentional and leans in on, "I am worthy to be in this meeting and contribute to this team."

She has some ideas on how one starts to build their brand, either at the beginning of their profession or to those that may be reassessing their brand mid-career. Here are four that she has highlighted which have made the difference as her career progressed:

Deep Expertise

To succeed in sales and delivery of professional services in the utilities industry, Susan had to become a SME in the power industry, which includes a deep knowledge of generation, transmission, distribution and customer operations, including understanding the technical aspects of the products and services offered by her firm, regulatory frameworks in each of the service territories her prospect utility serviced and emerging trends such as robotics and AI. She has cultivated a deep knowledge and developed a reputation for her expertise which is a crucial component of her personal brand.

Mature Resilience

Overcoming gender biases and stereotypes has required immense resilience. Susan, in her sales and delivery roles, has had to face many challenges, but she persevered and remained committed to her goals. Her determination has not only led to personal success but has also paved the way for other women entering this industry. That knowledge and desire to help other women in this field is a major reason for her being a part of this book.

Effective Communication

Effective communication is at the heart of successful sales in utilities. Women who have built strong personal brands in this sector excel in articulating complex concepts in a relatable manner.

Susan has lofty expectations and leads with hard transparency, not only with her clients but also with her staff and employees. Leaders, not just women, need to be comfortable with conveying bad and good news. Susan has weekly 'two-minute,' real-time feedback with her staff. She has found that people really do want to know how they're doing and what they can do to improve their performance.

Relationship Skills

The utilities industry relies heavily on relationships, whether it's with clients, regulatory bodies or internal teams. Women in sales have understood the significance of relationship building and have made it a core element of their personal brand. They are known for their ability to foster trust and collaboration. Susan understood that need for relationship building from the start. Whether it's delivering speeches to peers or clients, sharing professional victories on LinkedIn, mailing birthday cards or sending texts just to ask for help – relationship management in your career is predominant. If there is one thing that really must be front and center in building a brand, it's making sure that you convey a caring attitude and nurture every relationship. Make every interaction with people pleasant and remember that what you say and do reflects your brand, not the project you sell or deliver.

"People have to know that you care." – Susan Lynch

```
┌─────────────────────────────────────────┐
│        Susan's Brand Attributes           │
│   ❖  Resiliency                           │
│   ❖  Relationship Orientated              │
│   ❖  Transparency                         │
│   ❖  Utility Knowledge                    │
│   ❖  Exceptional Good Energy              │
└─────────────────────────────────────────┘
```

Final Thoughts

As Susan reflects, she attributes her career longevity to the people aspect of the consulting role.

Whether she is mentoring the next generation behind her or helping her clients understand and use their newly implemented system, every day brings fresh and interesting challenges. Being a consultant has been one of her life's greatest gifts. She hopes that her legacy is one of people knowing she cared that she showed up, and she used every day to deliver and foster excellence.

Dedication

This chapter is dedicated to Charlie Johnson, a steadfast partner and cherished friend to both Susan and me since 2000. In mid-2024, we received the somber news that Charlie was gravely ill and were urged to call him for what would be our final farewells.

Susan and I were privileged to speak with him and express our deep appreciation for his significant impact on our careers. I shared with Charlie that I was authoring a book celebrating women's achievements, with Susan Lynch featured prominently in one chapter. His reaction was one of sheer joy. However, upon learning that Susan had honored him as a mentor, he fell silent. It was only when I further revealed that he would be commemorated in the Library of Congress that he found his voice again.

His parting words were heartfelt: "Thank you, Connie. Please convey to Susan that her acknowledgment of me as a mentor, coupled with your dedication to writing a book that attributes some of her success to me, is the most meaningful accolade I've ever received in my professional life." With that, our conversation ended, and I was left with the emotional realization that I would never hear his voice again.

Chapter Highlights	Description
Industry Context	Utilities industry with historical gender diversity challenges.
Brand Evolution	Shift from no brand focus to understanding brand as an emotional client connection.
Superpower	Exceptional good energy that attracts and retains great consultants and clients.
Kryptonite	"Ultimate imposter syndrome," combating self-doubt and building self-worth.
Deep Expertise	SME in power industry, understanding technical aspects, regulatory frameworks, and emerging trends.
Mature Resilience	Overcoming gender biases and stereotypes, demonstrating determination and paving the way for others.
Effective Communication	Articulating complex concepts relatable, providing real-time feedback, and leading with transparency.
Relationship Skills	Fostering trust and collaboration, managing relationships as a core element of the personal brand.
Personal Touch	Sending birthday cards, texts, and maintaining pleasant interactions to reflect the brand.
Brand Advice	Care and nurture every relationship, as it reflects your brand beyond the projects you sell or deliver.

Susan Lynch is a native Floridian and lives in Orlando with her husband, Ty and family. She currently works as a managing director for Accenture in the Oracle practice. More about Susan can be found on LinkedIn at https://www.linkedin.com/in/susanclynch/

Chapter 8:
Michelle Fay
Partner at Guidehouse

From the Author:

I met Michelle Fay at CS Week in 2001. She was standing in the Aclara booth in the CS Week Exhibit Hall. At the time, Aclara was a little-known company that was competing in the advanced metering infrastructure (AMI) space. She was selling smart metering software, communication tools, sensors, controls and professional services.

AMI was not a well-known concept, and Michelle spent her time explaining why a smart meter company was exhibiting at a customer service conference. But there she was, standing the entire time with a big smile on her face and details about her product line always in mind.

Later, I met her again in Boston when I interviewed with Bridge Energy. She was gracious and professional, and even though I didn't proceed with that job, I followed her career progression on LinkedIn. Bridge was acquired, and she left and went to work at Navigant, now known as Guidehouse. I have watched her over the years and seen her professional growth to a senior, well-respected and knowledgeable partner. She has many publications to her credit and is a speaker on the utility thought-leadership circuit. She has been a lady to watch, and it is this author's belief that the best is yet to come for her. Here is her story. – C.T.C.

Leadership and Personal Work History

Michelle Fay started her journey after graduating in 1995 from Boston College's Carroll School of Management in Accounting and Information Systems. With her degree in hand, she joined Price Waterhouse (PW). She spent her first two years in public accounting, and there she studied and passed her Certified Public Accountant (CPA) test. After passing her accounting certification, she worked in financial audits, mergers and acquisitions and initial public offerings.

After a successful tenure, she transferred to the Management Consulting practice in 1997. At the time, PW was seeing high growth in Enterprise Resource Planning and needed consultants that were trained in both accounting and programming, an odd combination for anyone. Michelle knew both. She was immediately trained in Oracle Financials and was ready to be assigned to a project. In contrast to her time in accounting, there were very few women in consulting.

While waiting for an assignment that would use her Oracle knowledge, she got a call from a partner inquiring about her ability to write code. She said she did in fact know how to do so and soon was booked on a flight to Chicago. Her first consulting assignment was to program the account module of a gas management system for a utility. It was there that Michelle decided on a career in energy, a sector where she realized consistency and sustainability from the first project.

In 2001 when Michelle wanted to get married and start a family, she took a step back from traveling and went to work for Nexus Energy Software. Later acquired by ESCO Technologies, Nexus Energy Software merged with two AMI companies to become Aclara. She spent the next 11 years managing the professional services organization, and it was there that she was promoted to her first tenure as vice president.

When she first started with this group, the organization was small and had about 35 people. When she left, the company had grown to more than 2,000 employees.

On the software side of Aclara, there were a few women but not as many as in the public accounting space. On the engineering side of the company, the team was made up exclusively of men.

Once, she recalled being in a utility in which she was meeting with the client's technical team to discuss the professional services needs for implementing the Aclara software. Michelle asked her male manager to attend that meeting as well. The entire utility's technical team was men, and when questions arose, they were directed to her manager. After the manager deflected four of five questions to her (and she answered), one would think they would start asking her directly. They did not. That was 2008.

In 2012, she joined a small start-up utility consulting company, BRIDGE Energy Group. The company had about 25 people at the time, and she was the only woman on the executive team. She was there for seven years and did everything from large, complex program delivery to staffing and operations.

In 2019, BRIDGE was sold to Accenture. She chose not to join Accenture and instead was hired by Navigant. The day before she started, she was told that Navigant was purchased by Guidehouse. The company has grown from 7,000 consultants to more than 17,000 in less than five years. She is the industry solutions lead for the Energy Sustainability and Infrastructure segment, in which she manages a large team of about 400 people. Her career path has led her to this point, but she will add that each job has taught her a valuable lesson on how to lead. One does not magically jump from college to a corner office. It takes persistence, hard work and great performance.

In her 29-year career, she has never worked directly for a utility, instead providing consulting services to them. Her role as a consulting partner providing services evolved out of circumstantial opportunities. She did not have a vision board or a grand plan. She liked solving complex issues and providing positive impact. She worried less about her titles and more about successful projects. Michelle has been embraced by all who work with her. She has been helped along the way mostly by her male superiors. Opportunities would often present themselves, ones that she lacked confidence she could perform. In the end, however, she found she could. And her career progression shows that.

Career Foundation

Michelle has built her career on 'showing up' and delivering quality work on time and on budget. She admits to having help along the way. She has been surrounded by colleagues and management that had confidence in her before she had it in herself. At a project in Texas, a partner asked her to take a management role, even though she was only four years into her career. She feared she would fail, but her manager had left, and leadership tapped her. She was terrified of the prospect, having never done project financials and managing a team, but the partner was confident in her ability. And she was successful. Up until 2010, Michelle observed that men led the projects. She also noted that utility leadership was male dominated.

Building her career foundation, Michelle tapped into role models and mentors. Michelle shares proudly that her advocate and role model is her dad. He has been her biggest supporter, often telling her that she can do and be anything she wants to be.

Her father was a serial entrepreneur. His first venture was to purchase cows for the family's farm when he was a teenager. He had a high risk-high reward mentality, and he never let the lack of education or finances hold him back. When she thinks of him and his message to her as a young child, she immediately thinks of ways to succeed.

Michelle considers herself to be fortunate to have male and female mentors and role models throughout her career. Early on, two men in leadership roles served as her mentors. They took time to collaborate with her and develop career plans and progressions. Additionally, one mentor and a mother of four helped her learn the art of work and home life balance.

When asked about building a team under pressure, Michelle feels that leading by example is key. That has always been a foundational element in her career, and she never asks her team to do something that she is not willing to do herself. Additionally, she has tried to ensure she has held most positions that now report to her, because she feels it is important to know what those roles entail.

While at Aclara, Michelle and her team worked late nights and early mornings, performing software releases at odd hours. Michelle's mantra was: If her team was in working, then she was there too. Whether it was sending out client communications, helping to debug a coding error, getting bagels and coffee, whatever it took, no matter how small or insignificant; it was always important to keep everyone focused.

Another important career foundation principle of Michelle's is learning not to overshadow your team and allow each other, management and staff, to shine. Michelle is quick to point out, "When in an interview, one needs to say 'I;' however, when celebrating success, one needs to say 'We,' because it is always a team effort!"

When Michelle faces objection, she has had to learn to take the emotion out of the situation and instead look at data and facts. If facing a difficult discussion that Michelle fears could escalate, she finds that bringing data to the discussion takes the emotion out of the conversation. Michelle likes to focus on the facts.

She believes that her career has been enhanced by following important principles about her work ethic and teams. The importance of showing up, tapping into role models and mentors, leading by example and celebrating success is fundamental for good team dynamics. When discipline and guidance is required, working with data to drive fact-based discussions usually works to assuage a tough conversation.

> *"When in an interview, one needs to say 'I;' however, when celebrating success, one needs to say 'We,' because it is always a team effort!"* **– Michelle Fay**

Delivering Exceptional Client Service – Team Development

When developing a team, Michelle concentrates on culture since team dynamics will determine how well her company delivers exceptional client service. She focuses on six areas when it comes to culture:

1. **Demand integrity**. It's important to have personal expectations and uphold commitments.

2. **Put people first** (both clients and employees). Leading with empathy and getting to know your staff will help you relate and understand what your team may be going through on a personal level. Celebrate career (and personal) milestones, take care of those who are struggling and understand that people are our greatest assets.

3. **Embrace diverse perspectives**. Surround yourself with various thoughts and ideas, different backgrounds, genders, ethnicities, even finances.

4. **Encourage collaboration**. The whole is greater than the sum of the parts, so dig in and build a team that works for something greater than themselves.

5. **Tackle the tough issues head on**. As Michelle likes to say, "Get the skunks on the table!" She means: If you have a problem that stinks, bring that issue forth early and address it, so it doesn't get worse later.

6. **Keep the end client in mind** when developing the team. Utility clients have changed over the years, and vendor partners have had to change the way we support them. There used to be a one directional flow of energy from utility to consumer. Today, the notion of a 'prosumer and energy transformation' has evolved, where there is a change in expectations from the customers, back to the utilities. The energy business is in a state of rapid transformation. Energy does not flow one way anymore, rather consumers are increasingly adopting distributed energy resources like solar. These customers are not only consuming power but producing energy and are often referred to as 'prosumers.' Utilities are working to meet these increasing consumer demands with investments in technology and data

analytics. Vendors and consulting partners serving these utilities have had to change how we hire and develop teams. As technology advances and additional data becomes available, analytics are becoming increasingly important. Data scientists are now an integral part of teams.

Utilities also used to operate in silos. Now, they are beginning to be more integrated. So, when Michelle and her team are asked to solve the impact of renewables on the energy grid, she needs to bring in diverse staff with different disciplines. Today's questions can't be answered with one type of talent. One can't answer questions with one team. The teams must be large and more diverse to answer more complex questions.

The attributes of hiring consultants in 2024 are different than when Michelle started her career. Consultants right out of college are like 'shiny little pennies full of optimism.' Looking for intangibles from this talent pool, Michelle homes in on where they would fit into the culture she is trying to build. Where are their values? Do they have intellectual curiosity and the excitement to learn new things? Are they looking for a job or do they want to build a career? Each day, we in consulting are faced with new challenges, especially with the energy transition, so if the interviewee is incurious, this is an extremely hard job. Michelle hires for longevity and looks for loyalty. A large part of her culture is staying power, and even though she looks for different perspectives, she wants team culture.

Despite the most careful of plans, building a team can also come with adversity and failures. Adversity is something that all professionals face sometime in their careers. Michelle felt it earlier and credits it for ensuring she is better prepared and skilled as a leader by delivering on her commitments, using data and building great teams. That said, Michelle feels it's how you overcome adversity that creates those leaders.

Failure also comes with the job. Early in her career, she would dive into a project, thinking that she had all the answers. She would produce the plan and direct her team to execute it. As such, she did not inspire her team; she mandated and demanded. Over the years, she learned an especially important lesson: one must inspire the team to think to get things done. Now, she gathers perspectives before starting the plan. Building a team means one must build trust, and over the years she has learned to let them build the plan!

Building a Brand

Like many women of Michelle's era, building a brand is not something that she did purposefully early in her career. She doesn't enjoy speaking roles at conferences, conducting interviews or being profiled on LinkedIn; however, Michelle recognizes that this is an important aspect to the role of being a consultant.

She spends time reading the trade magazines, going to seminars and speaking to utility industry leaders to make sure she is current and engaged in her clients' concerns. She spends time authoring white papers and speaking at conferences now because she wants the industry to perceive her as a thought leader. She has been published in *Power Utility Fortnightly*, LinkedIn, and she speaks regularly at Grid CONNEXT.

The real brand that she wants to be known for is establishing strong and lasting client relationships. Ironically, the more senior one becomes in a consultancy such as Guidehouse, the further away from the client you become. One must make a concerted effort to keep in front of clients and make those touchpoints a priority. Developing both professional and personal reasons to contact each other makes those important relationships easier to maintain.

Michelle reflected on one client scenario. There were challenges on the company's project led by a senior executive, but she had developed a good relationship with him by providing excellent delivery. He went on to another company but remembered her going the extra mile to ensure she completed the project, even though it was troubled. He remembered and asked her to once again be a part of a new project at his new company. Her lesson was particularly important: maintain a positive connection, and what you start, finish well. Your brand is bigger than the company at the top of your business card.

When asked about her Superpower, Michelle is proud of her ability to build teams that can move mountains and to align her team for solving big challenges. She admits her Kryptonite is her inability to change course once on a path. To mitigate this, Michelle monitors herself and asks for feedback from her team to make sure she is being open to diverse ideas that might not be her own.

As one gets more senior in the market, a seat on an advisory board can go a long way to building and maintaining one's brand. Michelle is a member of GridWise Alliance, part of her utility industry brand, and Upward Women, a networking group to help executive women advance their careers. Both help women as utility professionals develop into leadership positions.

When asked about advice to young women that are starting to build their brand, Michelle advises them to think about it early in their career. Her advice? Do something that you are excited and enthusiastic about. Be authentic and make sure you have a high level of integrity. Areas of focus or industry will come into view over time, so stay patient and don't let anything be out of reach.

Michelle's Brand Attributes

- ❖ Authentic
- ❖ Confident in abilities
- ❖ Client Focused
- ❖ Thought Leader
- ❖ Dedication to future generations

"A 'lady to watch', Michelle has established herself as one of the prominent leaders in our industry. Michelle's 'showing up' leadership style really reflects in her hands-on, client focused, people first and result oriented way of doing things, achieving the best outcomes for her clients and team. She sets high standards for anyone that works with her, but even higher ones for herself, leading the challenges by example. After a recruitment effort of more than a year (!), I was fortunate to have Michelle join our leadership team at Guidehouse, where she excelled and build the best industry solution team in the world. Over the years I have been so impressed with her leadership and personal attributes. The way she achieves the highest results while taking care of the development of her team is some of the best I have seen. She is a people person at heart and besides changing the industry, she is dedicated to developing the future generation of leaders which our industry so desperately needs."
- Jan Vrins, Partner at Navitas Advisory

Final Thoughts

Michelle would like her legacy to be remembered as one that contributed to the utility industry and as a person that helped to transform the industry. She hopes the teams that she has built and continues to build have learned from her so they too can build great teams that will continue the legacy and continue to deliver on the energy transition.

As far as attracting and retaining women in utilities, she wants to think broader than this industry. Her daughter's perspective is extremely different than Michelle's was at her age. It would never occur to her daughter that there are jobs and opportunities that she could not apply for and not qualify to be hired. The legacy Michelle is leaving allows next generations to have more opportunities than she did.

Chapter Highlights	Description
Person Branding Approach	Initially passive, now proactive in building a brand as a consultant.
Public Engagement	Authoring white papers, speaking at conferences, being published, and participating in interviews.
Industry Focus	Utility industry, staying current with trade magazines, seminars, and industry leader discussions.
Brand Perception Goal	To be perceived as a thought leader in the utility industry.
Key Achievements	Published in Power Utility Fortnightly, regular speaker at Grid CONNEXT.
Core Brand Value	Establishing strong and lasting client relationships.

Client Relationship Strategy	Maintaining visibility and touchpoints with clients, developing professional and personal connections.
Notable Client Experience	Successfully completed a troubled project, leading to repeat engagement with a senior executive.
Professional Development	Member of GridWise Alliance and Upward Women, contributing to the utility industry and women's executive advancement.
Superpower	Building high-performing teams and aligning them to solve significant challenges.
Kryptonite	Difficulty in changing course once a path is chosen, countered by seeking team feedback.
Advice to Others	Start building a brand early, focus on authenticity and integrity, be patient, and keep all options open.

Michelle lives in Boston with her husband Peter, son Sean (20), daughter Michaela (17) and two dogs Peanut and Harley. More information about Michelle can be found on LinkedIn at https://www.linkedin.com/in/michelle-fay-205895/

Chapter 9:
Beth Kearns
Founding Partner and CEO of Triniti Consulting

F*rom the Author:*

I met Beth Kearns in 2005 when she worked at Lodestar, a company that sold utility software for settling the market, meter data management and complex billing. While there, Lodestar sold its Meter Data Management (MDM) system to a major Southeast region utility, and later Lodestar was sold to Oracle where I was the regional account representative. That utility was also one of my clients, and it was my job to support the new MDM system.
At that time, I knew nothing about MDM other than I knew I needed help.

Since Beth had previously run Lodestar's Professional Services Group, I called on her to help me with managing an extraordinarily complex project and demanding client. We worked closely together, and she helped educate me on the product, which even today I still know little about. She was kind, patient, gracious and certainly knowledgeable in an area where I had to stay one step ahead trying to maintain my client relationship. Beth was well-respected and still enjoys the respect of peers and even competitors. She helped me support the utility while transferring knowledge about this product suite with our every encounter.

After leaving Lodestar (prior to Lodestar's acquisition by Oracle), she went to work for a small company, Red Clay Consulting. There, she rose through the ranks quickly. She had the support of her past clients and continued support from Lodestar but on a smaller scale.

A few years later, she took a leap of faith, left Red Clay and started her own Minority/Woman Owned Enterprise, Triniti Consulting, where she became its chief executive officer.

I have personally witnessed this entire transformation of her and her career. It is that journey that demanded that she be included in this book. She has built a tremendous firm and recruited, retained and promoted excellent consultants.

She has made a great impression on me and many other women like me. (Not to mention the thousands of dollars I have spent on Christian Louboutin shoes because of her!) I hope you enjoy her story as much as I have enjoyed writing it. – C.T.C.

Leadership and Personal Work History

Beth Kearns started her career in utilities in a unique way. She studied as an undergraduate at the University of Houston, then earned her master's in Math from the Georgia Institute of Technology. A career fair at Georgia Tech introduced her to the world of consulting, and with her first glimpse she was sold on the idea of flying around the world, working on a laptop and advising clients on things she knew nothing about.

After completing her master's degree, she joined American Management Systems (AMS) in Fairfax, VA, as the first step in her professional career. Within AMS, she joined a new group as a developer and business analyst that focused on utilities. Because her degree was in math and not programming, she had to work harder to understand the ins and outs of development within applications for utilities. Solving business problems with technology became a passion for Beth immediately during her first assignment. She loved the thrill of finding not just any solution but the *best* solution.

She worked her way up through the organization performing all facets of implementation roles – developer, analyst, functional lead and project manager. While she had never worked directly for a utility, at AMS she worked within a larger consulting organization and later moved to a consulting group within a software firm. Because she experienced both consulting for a professional services firm and a software firm early in her career, she developed empathy for both sides and a unique perspective (as well as confidence) on how to be a great partner to all parties involved in an implementation.

After four years of steady domestic and international travel, she had grown weary of being a 'road warrior.' Without a plan, she left AMS, took time off and travelled around Italy, considering her next career move.

Focused on remaining in the utility consulting space but looking to gain experience working directly for a software vendor, she engaged with Lodestar. At the time, Lodestar was beginning to build out a professional services organization, and she'd gained experience working with two mentors at Lodestar during her time at AMS. One of the highlights of her career with both AMS and Lodestar was her leadership in the development of efficient implementation processes and procedures for their utility software. To her credit, Beth was recognized and rewarded at Lodestar, quickly rising in her six-year career there to run the services group during the last two years of her tenure.

At that time, Lodestar was being courted (and was eventually sold) to Oracle Utilities. Beth was used to a small firm, so she stepped out of Lodestar and subsequently out of the industry to a firm named TalentQuest, where she spent a year. Boredom set in quickly without the fast-paced, travel-laden consulting work for utilities, and she started considering her options. During her time out of the industry, another firm had been wooing her to join their team. As a small consulting company that had partnered with Beth during her time at Lodestar, they knew that she was a perfect fit. Beth made the move to join Red Clay Consulting to lead their team implementing the Oracle products suite. After five successful years growing the business from three people to 50, it was once again time for her to move on. During her time at Red Clay, she was treated well, and leadership allowed her to build a practice with little to no oversight.

"Maybe they made my head too big, maybe I was naïve," she wondered, but Beth didn't think twice before leaving to start her own company, Triniti Consulting, from scratch.

> *"Being a good partner is about making sure you are being fair to the people you represent and not harming anyone, regardless of whether they are your employee, your software partner, your customer or your implementation partner."*
> **- Beth Kearns**

In hindsight, Beth realized she had no idea the magnitude of the task she had undertaken, particularly the day-to-day operations behind the scenes that don't involve helping utility clients solve problems. But she did know she wanted to do things differently than she had at her prior company; she had learned from her mistakes. She knew she wanted to ensure that relationships were front and center for her new firm to enable and focus on continuous improvement in her people and her client engagements. Beth had a vision: Take great care of her employees so they could take amazing care of their customers. She wanted a uniquely different competitive landscape within Triniti. Instead of individuals succeeding at the expense of others and being driven to compete with one another, she wanted a true team culture where everyone succeeded or failed as a team, where no one succeeded because someone else in the firm failed. And finally, the most critical component of building Triniti was putting an extremely high value on building real, not superficial, relationships with her clients. Relationships that matter are what matter to her. Beth felt as if her teams should be in the trenches solving problems together, never pointing blame at partners, each other or leadership.

She'd had the privilege of working at and building so many different types of consulting organizations within larger consulting firms such as AMS, the consulting arm of a software vendor such as Lodestar and the small consulting firm, Red Clay. With those experiences, Beth owned deep knowledge and perspective about how to best serve her partners, her customers and her employees. She thinks this is the key to her success. Because of this experience, Beth formed Triniti with a focus on building partnerships with clients to solve problems together. To do that, she needed to get personal and really get to know them as people. She focused on those relationships as she strategically tackled business development and growth, and it has helped her successfully 'break the glass ceiling.'

Career Foundation

As Beth reflected on building her early career and professional foundation, she has gathered various pieces of advice and guidance along the way that helped define how she shaped her career. Like most women in this era, she felt different than those around her. She didn't find anyone, woman or man, who represented that end goal of her career or checked enough boxes to be someone she wanted to emulate. So, she followed patterns formed in childhood and forged her own way, figuring it out as she went along and making her own unique path while remaining true to herself and her values.

Early in Beth's life, her mother told her that she could be absolutely anything she wanted to be when she grew up. She encouraged Beth's individuality in all aspects, such as crazy fashion, wild haircuts and attending summer school, even though she didn't need to. Her mom had the vision, believed in Beth's potential and knew that her job was to facilitate, encourage and believe.

Learning from her mother (as well as early in her career), Beth has always been a big believer in leading by example. That includes doing the work with the team alongside them, not for them. This illustrates to the entire team that everyone should help each other and that no one is above getting their hands dirty. In fact, Beth said, "When push comes to shove, I can jump in and write code. Honestly, no one really wants that, but I could and would." As someone who wants to get things done quickly, it can often be frustrating to slow down and give people the opportunity to gain experience and grow, to not do it for them. But she passionately believes in helping people advance alongside and beyond you, not leaving people behind.

As she sees her people grow, both professionally and personally, Beth reflected on her own mentors throughout her career. Although she did not participate in a formal mentoring program, Beth was deliberate in studying women leaders fail and succeed, and she used this insight to mold her own leadership style. Most learnings came from perceived failings with the most memorable being,' Don't be yourself. Play the game,' which turned out to be a lesson that Beth vehemently rejects.

Throughout her career, most of her mentors in the utilities industry were men because until recently women leaders were few. She found women leaders on the client side of consulting in customer service departments, billing and accounting. She luckily had an abundance of men to thank for guiding her along the way and a handful of women on the client side who truly impacted her.

To support building personal relationships and providing mentoring, she calls each person on her team at least once a month to catch up. Understanding where each person is coming from better enables her to support them in their career goals and day-to-day work. Of course as Triniti Consulting continues to grow, that exercise will be harder to execute, but it remains an aspiration for any executive growing a brand that is dependent on relationships.

Delivering Exceptional Client Service – Team Development

Four to five years ago, Beth and Triniti went through a rebranding exercise. One of the first qualities the consultant suggested was to decide on the firm's culture. Together, they explored whether a culture should be defined from the top down or expanded from what the organization had become. She felt strongly that leadership should identify culture, aligning with the values she felt from the inception of Triniti. To that end, they worked together to get the values down on paper, prioritized, defined and elaborated on within the framework of the following key principles:

Primary Values

1. **Authenticity**. Having rejected the advice early in her career to 'play the game,' authenticity was the number one value that Beth wanted for Triniti. Be yourself. Bring your whole self to work and be true to yourself.

2. **Drive**. It's great to be who you are, but you must work hard too. It's not up to just a handful of people. Everyone on the

team needs to bring this key component and achievement to the table.

3. **Humility**. When you combine authenticity and drive without humility, you can easily create a monster. To promote the team spirit and vibe that is Triniti's brand, balancing those characteristics with humility is critical.

As she looks to expand her brand and her business, Beth holds these values in the forefront of her mind and evaluates everyone that she recruits to the team against them. Of course, new hires must have the right functional and technical skills for their roles, but values are the most important attributes evaluated after those skills. She expects her clients to support and hold similar values as well. When the Triniti team and the client's team are in the trenches in a tough project, there needs to be mutual respect based on authenticity, drive and humility to get things done. Those core values are paramount to her and her company's success.

Of course, building a successful team didn't come without failures, and like all of us, every single 'failure' she experienced has made Beth who she is today, so much so that she often repeats, "If you aren't failing, you aren't trying." She's proud of having failed because it means that she keeps putting herself out there and trying something new or different. Her biggest failure, at least as a leader, has been in finding someone who has a similar drive and passion for the business that she has created. She needs someone to take over the reins of the business once she decides to depart and has been through several seconds-in-command with no luck yet. She has found it difficult to find someone that is curious enough and driven enough to not only understand the complexities of running, maintaining and expanding a small business with the willingness to jump in and do whatever it takes to make it successful. From the outside, most people think being the CEO is glamourous travel, fancy dinners and conferences with little purpose. In fact, it's long days and nights, hard work like understanding the nuances of detailed contracts and requests for proposals or solving challenging human resource issues. She says, "It's figuring out the things that no one is around to figure out and, more importantly, just getting it done." No or failure is not an option for Beth. One day though, she has dreams of finding the right person to take over and let her retire to a life on the sea or in France or on the sea in France.

Building a Brand

Beth's entire personal and professional brand has been built on building relationships. In fact, she started developing her brand the first day of her undergraduate program, continued through graduate school, her first job and finally by establishing Triniti. She remains focused on this quality every day and encourages everyone to do the same. "A large part of your brand is your integrity, your reputation and the team members' reputations who stand around you. Protect your integrity and reputation," she advises, "and never settle for less than what you want your brand to be."

To watch Beth in action, you would think her ability to establish and nurture strong relationships with her clients and employees came easily to her. The fact is: it did.

Beth's strongest attribute is that she genuinely cares about people. She admits 'cheating' a little after an introduction by writing down meeting notes, so she can remember it later. "It's just natural that people appreciate it when you remember to ask about their child who just graduated, the pet that was sick or remember birthdays and anniversaries," Beth says. In this way, she wants those around her to feel special. In fact, in one meeting it's clear Beth wants to know you on a personal level. It's not all about business; it's about the person standing in front of her. When asked how to build a strong and lasting relationship, she says, "Vulnerability and honesty are key. There is a professional level of vulnerability you can share with others to keep true to yourself while being open and honest."

When asked about her most successful client relationship that demonstrates her brand, one she still has and maintains, Beth reflects on her first project as a consulting project manager at PEPCO (now part of Exelon). She remains personal friends with clients that she worked with on that project back in 1999 and the consulting project manager for whom she first worked. To Beth, the 25-year friendship she has maintained to this day is the very definition of a successful client relationship. In fact, that project manager from 1999 is her current sales executive at Triniti. All this came about because Beth was curious, cared, paid attention and was authentic, vulnerable and honest. Today, they have a great working relationship (as well as personal), and it demonstrates who Beth is as a professional.

Excellent work can also help build a good brand. Beth won and delivered a project for Minnesota Power and Superior Water, Light and Power (ALLETE) that directly led to clearly tangible benefits for the client which, in turn, bolstered her professional brand.

The project was implemented based on fostering strong relationships between Triniti Consulting and ALLETE so that both organizations could easily demonstrate a 'one team' concept, showing there was no way to differentiate between ALLETE and Triniti personnel when you entered a project team room. This project was the first to implement Oracle Utilities' Customer to Meter (C2M) system and utilize it in a new methodology designed with partnership and teamwork in mind. Everyone would succeed or fail together; there was no one person or entity winning alone. Out of this dynamic, Beth received the best compliment of her career from former ALLETE Customer Experience Transformation Manager Jeanne Atkinson who said, "This relationship between Triniti and ALLETE was hands-down the best partnership that I have experienced in my 34 years of doing project work."

Beth considers her Superpowers to be persistence and curiosity. She believes them to be secret, critical and essential to her success. The ability to be in polite but consistent contact, follow-up multiple times and not make the client irate takes special finesse. She also considers her competitiveness and drive to be Superpowers as well. She admits she wants to win, and she will not give up. Her only Kryptonite is boredom, but thankfully her curiosity keeps that at bay.

Beth's Brand Attributes

- ❖ Integrity
- ❖ Meticulous to detail
- ❖ "One Team" Mentality
- ❖ Deep Client Relationships
- ❖ Mentors of Strong Women

Final Thoughts

Beth's advice to anyone beginning their career, establishing a company or even starting over is this: "Remember that everything you do is your brand, so figure out who you are and be authentic to that. It's the best chance for it to 'stick.' Second, be ready to fight for it, and third, be ready to wear a lot of hats."

If you're a client-facing leader such as the women interviewed in this book, don't take no for an answer. If you're mentoring other women that are following you, remember what you wished you had when you were beginning your career and how that would shape the decisions you would have made (or not made). Just because someone wants to do things differently, doesn't make it wrong. And take some advice from Beth: "When you don't know what to do, just start."

When asked what she wants her legacy to be when she retires from the industry, it's simple: Beth wants the consultancies to make more space for and honor diversity, inclusion and authenticity.

Diverse thought is extremely important to the utility industry now, since without it we will keep solving problems the same way. As our problems grow, they change and become more complex, so must we, which demands a new world of creative thinking.

Few women make it long term in consulting; long hours and demanding travel take a toll. After a certain time, if they start families, women tend to leave the field. Beth is making it her goal to find a solution to keep women in consulting and show the world that utility consulting is a long-term, worthwhile profession, with a lifetime of great friends and rewarding professional relationships. To do this, she believes we need to make space for women with families, encourage work-life balance and bring our whole selves to work.

Chapter Highlights	Description
Foundation of Brand	Building and nurturing relationships from undergraduate days to establishing Triniti.
Core Focus	Maintaining integrity, reputation, and encouraging team members to do the same.
Relationship Building	Natural ability to establish and nurture strong relationships with clients and employees.
Personal Touch	Takes notes about personal details to remember and ask about later, making others feel special.
Approach to Relationships	Values vulnerability and honesty to build strong and lasting connections.
Longevity of Relationships	Maintains a 25-year friendship with a client from her first consulting project.
Professional Collaboration	Demonstrates a "one team" concept with clients, blurring the lines between company personnel.
Client Testimonial	Received high praise from ALLETE for the partnership with Triniti.
Superpowers	Persistence, curiosity, competitiveness, and drive.
Kryptonite	Boredom, which is mitigated by her natural curiosity.
Advice to Others	Protect your integrity and reputation, and never settle for less than your brand's potential.

Beth splits her time between Atlanta, GA and Nice, France, with her husband, Rodney and their two cats. More information can be found on her LinkedIn page at https://www.linkedin.com/in/bethkearns/ and https://www.linkedin.com/company/triniti-consulting-llc/

Chapter 10:
Laura Sciuto
Senior Manager at a Big Four Accounting Firm

From the Author:

I met Laura in 2019 when she joined my project at Consolidated Edison of New York (ConEd) as a part of the CORE implementation of Oracle Customer Care and Billing Customer Information System (CIS) Implementation project. CORE is the name ConEd calls their phenomenally successful CIS project. She was a manager in the People Advisory Services practice, responsible for OCM and Training and was paired (co-leads) with our client Orlando Hernandez, Change Management Department Manager, for this large transformation project that had been underway in some capacity since 2014, even earlier. Change was going to be huge across not only the entirety of the New York City workforce but also across ConEd's subsidiary, Orange and Rockland. Laura was special from the first meeting! She had a certain vibe, and I could tell that she was someone I wanted to keep not only on this account but in this industry. She is smart and precise; she has emotional intelligence beyond her years. I knew she could be a disciple.

There had been so many young women who had come and gone on this account. The challenge to attract women to work in the power and utility sector had been tough. All the others before her wanted to work in Automation or something more exciting. When the COVID Pandemic occurred, all the 'cool projects' stopped.

Now was the opportunity. I had to devise a plan! And Laura was a perfect candidate. Not only eager to learn, but she was also young enough to appreciate the position she encountered, a sustainable job in her home city of NYC in the middle of a pandemic. And so, she became my youngest profile.

I penned a book for women like Laura, and her persona is why she is highlighted in this book. I wanted to spark interest and at least have women (and men) explore the industry. She and women like her have Superpowers wanting to be discovered. Here is her unlikely story. As luck would have it, she began her career as a self-declared "brat." – C.T.C.

Leadership and Personal Work History

Laura graduated from the University of Pennsylvania in 2009 with a degree in Sociology and Hispanic Studies. In 2008, the summer before her junior and senior years, she interned with Macy's, and in classic Millennial fashion she hated it. After graduation, she was offered a low wage job in NYC; she turned it down, convinced she could *easily* find something better. Three days later the market crashed, Lehman Brothers imploded, and her parents chided her for being so shortsighted in turning down the job offer while wondering if their investment in her college tuition had been for nought. Desperate for money and being a self-proclaimed material girl (Laura self-describes as "shoe rich and cash poor"), she landed a job on a cruise ship selling luxury goods for a Louis Vuitton subsidiary. The crew was exciting and international, and she spent the winter of 2009–2010 cruising the Caribbean (and occasionally using her degree in Hispanic Studies), but soon she had to return to reality. In the summer of 2010, a personal connection who was a partner at the audit firm Deloitte offered her the opportunity to interview with Deloitte's Human Capital consulting practice. She was intrigued (and well-aware that she needed a 'real' job). She interviewed, accepted the job based out of New York City and spent two and a half years with Deloitte.

Her first project was at a large multi-national retailer as they transformed their finance operations globally; Laura was on the change and training workstream focused on finance in Mexico and Argentina. The workstream was responsible for all SAP training as part of this transformation; Laura was a training developer on the team.

In her role, she learned to develop and teach finance in SAP in Spanish. Even though when she started, she did not know most of what she was translating (her Spanish classes at Penn had unsurprisingly not focused on finance function vocabulary), she learned along the way. During the remainder of her time at Deloitte, Laura continued to work on large-scale, technology-focused transformations, primarily within the Consumer Products industry. In Laura's mind, this was the industry closest to the customer (or so she thought back then).

But she wanted to "save the world and solve for world hunger." Laura was 25 and felt she was not making a "positive impact" on the world, so she left consulting to become a journalist, where she felt she could have a voice on the topics that really mattered. Her first steppingstone appeared in 2013 in the form of an internship at the PBS NewsHour in Arlington, VA, where she would earn $8 per hour and submit her time on paper timesheets. Unfortunately, her constant suggestions that NewsHour might consider moving to an electronic time-keeping platform (it was 2013, after all!) combined with her (delusional) designs to hang out with Prince Harry (which she expressed to the Royal Press Secretary in an email from her PBS address) did not ingratiate Laura with her new employer.

Citing her for insubordination and the near implosion of an international incident (apparently interns emailing the Royal Press Secretary asking for an audience with Prince Harry was a big no-no), PBS immediately terminated Laura's employment. Her brief tenure in the DC area (along with her dreams of being a journalist) ended as she moved back to New York. She took another lackluster job at an executive recruiting and market research startup, and after about a year of that she decided she might need a bit more structure and guidance in her young life. She went back to what she knew and interviewed with consulting practices at the Big 4, and my firm Oracle seemed the best fit. The practice Laura joined, then called the People & Organizational Change Group within a Big 4 Advisory line of business, was structured and fully formed with room to grow. The people seemed intelligent, thoughtful and ambitious. That was September 2014. Laura had landed as a senior consultant and spent the next five years continuing to grow her skills as a change management and training consultant, primarily focused on large scale technology projects in consumer and consumer-adjacent industries (e.g., diversified industrial products). Laura was promoted to manager in 2017 and was moving along (unremarkably, she'll tell you) in her consulting career.

Never in a million years did Laura think she would find herself in the Power and Utilities industry, but then in 2019, Ryan Levine (one of her original interviewers from 2014) called and asked her to work on a project at Consolidated Edison, Inc. in NYC. She accepted for a number of reasons: Laura was already traveling every other weekend to Philadelphia for her Executive MBA program; the ConEd assignment offered a local role, and that role was a Change Management Lead; the opportunity granted her the chance to combine all the experiences she'd had to date into one. And then she fell in love with the Power and Utilities industry. The people were so diligent and motivated, the subject matter was stimulating, and most importantly the connection to the customer could not be more real. Laura realized this is where she belonged. She excelled in her role at ConEd, all the while growing her Power and Utilities industry knowledge and experience and was promoted to senior manager in 2021.

Career Foundation

Laura had a bit of a windy path to her current role, but each of those past positions (both within and outside of consulting) has one thing in common: she did not give up on moving forward. When one door closed, she looked for a crack in an open window. She was not afraid to move roles, to take chances on what she thought she should do next or to physically relocate. In 2024 during our interview period, Laura had decided that after nearly 14 years (save for her short 2013 stint in Arlington) and one long Pandemic in NYC, she needed a change, so she loaded all her possessions into storage and decided to test out three or four cities to see where she might want to live next. Packing up her apartment, her home for nine years, was daunting, but she had the support of her leadership. Laura also had the foundation of strong relationships with her clients, so she pursued the change. Laura's career foundation, like her nomadic living plan, has been built on faith and confidence that she could make things work out. The path might not be smooth, and the plan might have to be adjusted, but with enough focus and support from those around her Laura had been able to find her footing and ultimately drive to the right outcome.

Her career at her current company has been built on large technical transformational programs, and all her past experiences have given her business savvy and skills to do the technical day-to-day work and manage both client relationships and her teams. Over the course of her time in consulting, she continuously built on past roles and was able to add more responsibilities as she managed larger projects and bigger teams. She manages in every direction: upward with partners, laterally with peers and downward with staff. Finding her voice as a teammate and a team leader has been a long-term evolution for Laura. She believes that if a person wants success in consulting the key is teamwork. There is a need for hierarchy to provide structure and to make consulting's 'apprenticeship model' work, but the best ideas can and must come from anywhere on the team. Laura believes that, as one builds the foundation of a career, the fundamental rule is to be inclusive, as great ideas can come from anywhere at any time, and a smart leader understands and embraces that reality.

When asked about her mentors, she immediately cited her mother who worked in banking her entire childhood and retired when Laura was 16. Laura's mom showed her the importance of having a career and developing oneself as a professional.

At her current company, Laura deeply values the mentors she has. Her very first true mentor at our company, Sussan Chakamian, had a reputation for being intense and highly demanding of her teams. When Laura was assigned to Sussan's project in 2015, she figured it would be the end of her. Sussan, then a senior manager, was the first person Laura had ever encountered who really saw her for what she was and what she could be. She looked at her wholistically (your current work product, how do you carry yourself, what knowledge do you possess now, what do you need to know in the future and what are your goals as a professional). Sussan became Laura's mentor at the Big 4.

Laura's other key mentor is Ryan Levine, the partner at her current Big 4 accounting firm who interviewed her back in 2014 and staffed her on the ConEd project. "An example of the best the professional world has to offer, Ryan delivers the best for the firm and for his clients while also caring deeply about his people and working tirelessly for them," says Laura. Ryan taught Laura the two realities that she holds most dear to her understanding of consulting: 1. Win in the market. To do this, you must deliver the best and really be the best. Yes, it's projects and sales, but you don't get those if you don't 'know your stuff' and can't deliver results. 2. Your people are key. Surrounding yourself with good people, closely knowing the people you work with and being on the journey with them is essential.

> *"Thanks in large part to Sussan, and other key role models in her life, Laura has a 'we all elevate each other' mentality. Laura understands, too, that she is a mentor and role model to others. That fact can be simultaneously, rewarding, daunting and humbling."* - **Ryan Levine, Partner at a Big 4 Accounting Firm**

Laura uses her mentoring experiences with Sussan and Ryan to develop both personal and professional relationships with the people on her teams, and she cares about their success more than anything else. She considers that part of the consulting culture as "always paying it forward."

Developing Exceptional Client Service – Team Development

Laura describes the culture of her teams as concerned primarily with apprenticeship and people development. At the apex of her team development ethos is the mantra that client delivery is always top-of-mind and for what her team gets paid. Exceptional client delivery happens through collaboration, really working side-by-side and "being in it together." Exceptional delivery and collaboration happen at all levels of an organization, so Laura focuses on instilling in her teams the mindset of "leaving your rank at the door." According to Laura, "If you want all the glory for yourself, then consulting is not for you. If you want an environment of true teaming and delivery of the absolute best results, then consulting is for you."

When Laura and her team look for new consultants in the utility practice, she looks for a hungry, 'can-do' attitude. Her team's joke is that Laura moonlights in information technology (IT) support, as she is always trying to fix IT problems for her team members. She looks for that same mentality when hiring consultants, men or women. No matter age or experience, she wants to know, firstly, 'Do you want to be here?", because life is too short to collaborate with people who don't want to be team players, and secondly, "Do you want to learn to do what it takes to deliver? Do you have confidence in your ability, along with a willingness to learn? If you do, you are the right person to be a part of her team."

When asked about adversity from other women or men when growing in her career, she had a refreshing answer. "For me, this is not so relevant. The culture of adversity has significantly changed over the last few generations. It used to be a tight race to be a successful woman because there were very few in top positions. But now, that's not the case. If there are 10 top positions, women and men are seen as having an equal ability to fill them. "I don't feel the competition so much. I feel like the women who are the most senior are opening doors for the next generation because they'll need to retire one day, and they want someone who they know and trust to take their place," she explained. Laura believes others want her success, so she can be an example to the women following behind her.

Reflecting on my own 40 years in the industry, these statements from Laura were incredible to hear. After so many years of personal struggle with getting ahead and hearing about similar struggles from my peers, such a powerful statement that we are seeing women reaching back to help other women get ahead was both inspirational and rewarding. Laura's experience is a testament to the women leaders of today and their relentless focus on changing the culture they grew up in to make space for more women in this industry.

Laura was asked about a woman leader in 2024 who had affected her hope, resilience and success. To my surprise, she said, "It's you, Connie." Laura reflected that there had been many wonderful women in her career, but when she thought of women in Power and Utilities, she thought of me, Connie Carden. She explained, "You stand for what you believe in, Connie; you have staying power, and you have fun doing it." Laura went on, "You've provided many opportunities to help me grow through a direct hand in projects where you have influence and perspective, and you have been able to help me navigate experiences to achieve my goals."

Those comments were a complete surprise, as we rarely have any certainty around where and when we are making a difference. Laura's sentiments remind me that each day people are watching, and it's important that we all remember the image we are showing each other and the care we're giving to each other.

> *"Attracting women like Laura is a major reason for authoring this book. I know when I retire and leave the utility industry, I will leave my legacy in a better place than where I found it!"* -
> **Connie Carden**

Building a Brand

Back in the seventies and early eighties, Patty Bruffy, many of our contemporaries and I did not think about building a brand. However, building a brand has been ingrained in Laura's mind since she entered the workforce. In fact, it seems to have been a big focus area for Millennials and Gen Zs, a factor that has separated successful young professionals from the less successful. In Laura's case, it has always been a large part of her career and something she is extremely conscious of in the professional setting. How her actions speak for her and affect her life is not only relevant at work, but at this point in her life it's part of her personal existence too. Her brand is who she is.

A major part of Laura's brand is her client relationships which are built on always doing the right thing. Not only does she work to show her clients that she will do the right thing during the sales cycle, but she makes sure to carry that forward during delivery. And the most effective way to build rapport with the client is by showing them how Laura and her teams work, listening closely and delivering beyond their high expectations.

One example of a particularly successful client relationship and a testimonial to brand building is the relationship Laura has with Department Manager Orlando Hernandez, a 30-plus year employee at ConEd in New York City. When Laura started working on the CORE project, she and Orlando were "two in a box." Laura had the mindset that this was her time to decide if she was going to be a good consultant. If she was going to be a good one, she needed to prove it by delivering for Orlando and being there throughout the CIS implementation. She went all in, and as a result Orlando knew that even when things were tough, she was there for him, leading the team and driving their commitment to doing things the right way. Laura is proud that after spending four and a half years 'in the trenches' with Orlando and seeing the CIS program through to go-live and into stabilization, they delivered exceptional outcomes for ConEd and became close friends.

> *"Working closely with Laura Sciuto for over four years during our customer service system implementation, I witnessed her incredible talents firsthand in so many situations. Laura is extremely bright, articulate, professional, resourceful and engaging. What always impresses me is her ability to tackle any problem, issue or request, regardless of complexity or sensitivity, with the same level of drive to meet or exceed her client's expectations. I often complemented her for her 'photographic memory,' which she modestly denies, but she was my personal 'AI resource' to find an answer or solution quickly and accurately. Laura is an industry-wide leader in change management, training and business readiness strategy. She made me a better leader through our great working relationship and partnership, and I am so privileged to have been in the trenches with her during our historic and successful project."*
> **– Orlando Hernandez, ConEd**

When asked about her Superpower, Laura immediately suggested she was a great "joker" but didn't think her sense of humor should be her Superpower.

Unsure, she asked her colleagues for their thoughts. They suggested a trait that Laura raised herself throughout our interview; namely, she is relentless about doing what's right. She said that it's always important to her to understand what the most important right thing is to do, as sometimes there are multiple **right** ways to approach various situations and then pursue that chosen path.

When asked her Kryptonite, she quickly replied, "Self-doubt." Her own insecurities creep in often, and then she "crumbles." She expends a tremendous amount of energy taming these insecurities and sees a fine line between maintaining and projecting confidence versus over-compensating and coming across as arrogant.

When Laura gives advice to her colleagues and other young individuals, she does her best to collect everything she has learned into a few key messages. Firstly, she suggests that planning and having goals is great. Youngers always impress Laura with their focus on having personal and professional plans. At the same time, Laura's experience has shown her that it is equally important to have enough room for flexibility and to enable an evolution in the path you are taking. Open-mindedness is key, and Laura encourages people to, in pursuit of their plans, make sure they are as open and available as possible to do anything and everything while they have energy for it. Laura came to this realization a bit late in her late 20s-early 30s, and she hopes others can learn from her mistakes. She encourages people to be the person that people know would be willing to do anything (within reason, of course). And finally, she encourages people to seek out collaboration since results are always better when we're working together. She recommends not doing anything alone, instead always seeking out an exceptional team for thought partnership and support.

Laura's Brand Attributes

- ❖ Loyalty
- ❖ Relentlessness
- ❖ Reflectiveness
- ❖ Flexibility
- ❖ Goal Oriented

Final Thoughts

Laura wants to be remembered as someone who always focuses on doing what is right for the people who collaborate with her (more senior, peers and more junior), as well as clients she serves. Laura explained during our interviews, "There is no place in the world for aggressive mediocrity," and she applies that lesson to all facets of life, most of all the relationships she builds. She hopes the people around her will look back and say she cared about them, their success and their professional and personal goals. When she is more experienced and has worked longer in her field, Laura strives for the milestone that someone will say she lifted them up, "Like so many people have done for me."

Chapter Highlights	Description
Brand Awareness	Conscious of building a brand since entering the workforce, integral to personal and professional identity.
Client Relationships	Built on doing the right thing, maintaining integrity throughout the sales cycle and delivery.
Client Rapport	Demonstrated by listening closely to clients and delivering beyond expectations.
Successful Client Example	Strong relationship with Orlando Hernandez at ConEd, leading to exceptional outcomes and friendship.
Superpower	Relentlessness about doing what's right, with the ability to discern and pursue the best path.
Kryptonite	Self-doubt, which can lead to crumbling under pressure, managed by balancing confidence.
Advice on Planning	Emphasizes the importance of having plans and goals while maintaining flexibility for evolution.
Open-Mindedness	Encourages being open to opportunities and willing to take on various tasks.
Collaboration	Advocates for teamwork and collaboration for better results and support.
Personal Growth	Recognizes the value of learning from past experiences and sharing insights with others.

Laura lives in New York City and other cities across the country with her dog, Tater Sciuto. More information about Laura can be found at LinkedIn at https://www.linkedin.com/in/laurasciuto/

Chapter 11:
Connie Turner Carden
Author

F*rom the Author:*

I have revisited this final chapter numerous times, each iteration filled with the intent to write about more fascinating individuals. Consistently, I am urged to share my own career journey, the obstacles I've faced, the lessons I've learned and my progression through the years. Like many, I've grappled with "imposter syndrome" and have had to muster the strength to pick myself up and continue.

Since the onset of my career in 1983, I've battled a fear of public speaking. It's not the typical concerns about appearance—whether my hair is amiss, my dress too snug or my makeup too much or too little—that troubles me.

Rather, it's the fear that I have nothing of value to say, nothing that would capture an audience's interest. As you can imagine, writing the first nine chapters about women whose stories are eagerly anticipated was a task that seemed to complete itself. But writing about myself? That's an entirely different challenge. So, I've intentionally saved my story for last, and here it is. – C.T.C.

Leadership and Personal Work History

Born to Sarah Pruitt Turner and James Robert Turner on September 28, 1961, I entered the world as the child of 44-year-old parents in Eden, NC. When I was born, I already had a grown sister, Judi, born in 1939. So, from the beginning, I had two mothers or rather, a sister that was old enough to be my mother and a mother who was often mistaken as my grandmother. My experience growing up was just that small town. I dreamed of living in a big city. Every day I prayed to leave Eden. I wanted to see what the world could offer a small-town girl.

My father, a firefighter, devoted 34 years to the City of Eden, retiring in 1983 with a modest annual salary of $14,000. He also served as a fire truck driver, drawing on his military experience driving trucks for the Army. My mother, a self-taught florist, previously worked at Fieldcrest Mills on the cotton gin producing blankets. Harassed by her superiors, she left and reinvented herself in the floral industry. After my birth, she would bring me to work each day at her florist shop, where I quickly learned the art of customer service selling her floral creations. Her top weekly earnings were $200. No matter the money they made, my parents never let me go without anything I wanted.

My mother was my inspiration and who I wanted to be when I grew up. She was seventh of 14 kids, one of two girls with 12 brothers. My mother quit school in third grade to take care of her brothers and sisters. After she married my dad, she worked at Fieldcrest Mills making blankets for 30 years, sexually harassed for most of it but tolerated the oppression for the good of her family. She finally made a move and started her own business as a florist. She had no formal education (nor did my father), had no experience as a florist, but she was much happier. She read a lot, figured things out on her own, and soon she became the top-selling florist in Eden. I saw her career progress from the playpen until I became a young adult. I learned about customer experience at her knee. I learned patience by watching her. I learned everything good that I am from her. She encouraged me to go to college and take a chance on myself. She believed in me before I knew where my path would take me. And I imagined a long time ago that if she could do all she had accomplished with a third-grade education, then imagine what I could do with a college degree.

My family's singular goal for me was to attend college—a milestone neither of my parents with their limited formal education had reached. Every weekend, we visited my grandfather and his wife,

Dora. He had been a tenant farmer and because of his good nature, he was allowed to keep his home—a humble abode without electricity, complete with an outhouse adorned with the iconic crescent moon. It was my grandfather, Sandy, who taught me the worth of the family and our commitment to each other, rather than money, as a core value of my youth.

At the age of five, when I started first grade, my mother recounted the story of my birth. I had nearly died during delivery, but miraculously I survived. She saw this as a sign that I was destined for greatness. Over the years, she instilled in me the belief that I was intelligent, would attend college and would leave Eden behind. In 1979, after applying for and being accepted by many in-state colleges, I chose Appalachian State University, a small liberal arts college nestled in the North Carolina mountains.

In the summer of 1981, I faced the task of declaring my major. My father, though unfamiliar with the intricacies of college, advised: choose one major I loved to maintain my sanity and one I disliked so that I could challenge myself. I followed his advice and selected Marketing and Computer Science. Unbeknownst to him, I loved them both. Later, I added Management Information Systems and Psychology, as I loved college and my experience there.

In June 1983, I embarked on my career with Management Science America (MSA) in Atlanta, GA, a modest $120 million company which specialized in developing and selling Enterprise Resource Planning software and competed against the likes of McCormack & Dodge. (Both companies, MSA and McCormack & Dodge have since been absorbed into Infor, paving the way for today's multi-billion-dollar industry giants, Oracle and SAP.)

I was recruited by SVP of Sales Rick Page, also a North Carolina native, because I reminded him of home. He was an integral part of my early sales and services training, always reminding me, "Hope is not a strategy." He later authored a book of that same name. A true gentleman, Rick taught me the fundamentals of great customer service.

MSA was an exceptional workplace led by John Imlay, a former IBM employee who treated his staff like royalty. Monthly, he would welcome new hires, invite them individually on stage and present us with a blue Tiffany box containing a sterling silver lapel pin shaped as a key—a larger design for women, a smaller one for men. It was not until later that I understood the significance of that gift. We were encouraged to wear it while traveling to signify our affiliation with MSA and to remind us that "People are the key," a principle I still uphold. I proudly wear a Tiffany key necklace today to remind me of that significant life lesson.

After four rewarding years at MSA, I joined Price Waterhouse to implement the General Ledger software I had developed. In just four years, I had transitioned from a COBOL programmer to a software services engineer and now to a senior consultant at a Big 8 accounting firm — a rapid ascent that felt overwhelming at times. This was the moment that I understood the term, "over my skis."

In 1991, I became too closely aligned with a client, a misstep known as "going native." Consequently, I parted ways with the firm. That year was also a pivotal one in my personal life.

During my time at MSA in the mid-1980s, I encountered someone who seemed to be the ideal partner. He was in the business of selling ERP software, while my role was to implement it. He quickly began earning an annual income ranging from $200,000 to $400,000, whereas I consistently earned between the low and mid-forties. This disparity became glaringly obvious each tax season when he would compare the taxes on his income to my entire salary. As a result, I settled into the comfortable life of a 'pampered' 30-year-old without much thought for my own future. However, an epiphany struck me: I aspired to have both a career and a family, and I was eager to venture into sales myself. I believed I had a more amiable personality and could succeed just as he had.

But life had other plans. When I expressed my ambitions, I faced harsh criticism and was told that I couldn't manage the rejections inherent in sales. Ultimately, my path seemed destined to be a stay-at-home mother with two children. Our discussions about my career aspirations led to increased verbal hostility from him. The situation escalated to a physical altercation when he slapped me and hurled insults that I had never been subjected to. That was the final straw.

I made the decision to leave, to find my own strength; and I never looked back.

I recount this experience because many young women have inquired about how I achieved success. The answer is resilience. I was knocked down in a very real sense, but I stood back up. I want to convey to everyone that the journey to success can be obstructed by significant obstacles. Reflecting on that pivotal moment, I recognize how it profoundly influenced my life.

Later in 1991, I joined Amdahl as a software and hardware services engineer, selling professional services. Even though unplanned, it was serendipity because my resume now reflected software engineer, Big 8 consultant and most recently hardware engineer. It is also where I met my husband and partner, a man that made my life complete and my career soar. It was there that I also adopted my family.

The '90s brought the rise and fall of dotcoms, and after a few missteps, I found myself at Oracle Corporation in 1997, working in the State and Local practice in Florida. After securing several significant deals including selling Customer Information Systems to a water company, I was recruited by a partner at KPMG, Charlie Johnson. KPMG, then BearingPoint, was sold to PwC. I had already worked with Price Waterhouse earlier in my career and wanted something different. So, I returned to the software industry joining Oracle, focusing on selling utility software.

After many years selling to state and local entities, a change was in order. The transition from state and local to Investor-Owned Utilities (IOUs) at Oracle was a natural shift for me. The lack of control, the unpredictability of politics and the use of lobbyists was often challenging. I found working with IOUs was straightforward. I could add value, and I finally felt I had something to contribute.

Eventually, I joined IBM as a strategic account partner for utilities across the Southern US. While at IBM, I encountered a great firm which shared my values, and they offered me a job in the New England region. I moved to Boston and worked with two utilities, met lots of exceptional people and delivered many successful projects.

For the past decade, I've remained with that Big Four accounting firm since.

Career Foundation

I have learned many lessons over my 40-plus year career, and I continue to learn every day, including the importance of developing deep and appropriate client relationships, trusting my instincts, becoming transparent and mentoring. I have also learned what does not work. Saying yes to everyone, taking on too much responsibility, not taking chances and not believing in my abilities are just a few. One last and important lesson as a consultant is this: Remember the company at the top of your paycheck.

Maintaining a close but appropriate client relationship while ensuring you are representing the firm is an important principle. I learned that the hard way when I went native. "Going native" is when you are so tightly aligned with a client that you identify as the client and not as the consultant, causing you to alienate other colleagues. Eventually, that behavior will cause harm to you in your firm. It did to me, and I was fired. That harsh lesson has stayed with me, a mistake that I have not repeated.

Another valuable insight is that you never know where someone at the client site will end up - an intern today could be CEO tomorrow. Similarly, within your own company, an assistant programmer might one day become the CIO. Lesson learned? Be nice to everyone, regardless of their rank, as all of us aspire and some of us reach our goals faster than others. When you stay in the utility industry long enough, people will progress quickly, and a subordinate today could be your manager tomorrow.

I learned to trust my instincts on a project in 2005. I failed to persuade my firm's leadership to trust the good faith I had built with a client in West Palm Beach, FL. I had been travelling to the client for three years, to the point where the client thought we had secured more business than we had. Our firm was selected for a large project, and we were negotiating commercials. The client asked for a $100K reduction to meet our competition's pricing, but he assured me that he would sole source the next piece in two months, and we would get the $100K returned. My firm declined. I should have been more assertive. The project was lost, and the firm was eventually sold. Lessons from that experience are lasting.

Another great lesson is this: Be truthful, always. Transparency is the cornerstone of trust. Whether the news is good or bad, clients and teams will stand by you if you're honest. Remember, if you burn a bridge, be prepared to never cross it again and be at peace with that decision. Trust your gut—it's usually right. Most clients consistently characterized me with one phrase, 'We always know where Connie stands.' The sooner the client or my leadership knows the truth, the quicker they can plan a call to action. Time spent "sugar coating" the facts does not make them any easier; rather, it just delays the resolution. It is my experience that people trust people who solve problems, not cover them up.

Finding a mentor would have made my journey smoother. I've had many advisors since, but no true mentor. I aim to change that for other young women. Each month, I connect with six to seven women (and a few men) to offer guidance, support promotions and provide advice on challenging situations. I think mentoring these women has been my greatest contribution in the last 10 years. As my career ends, these conversations and seeing these women progress from rank to rank is my proudest accomplishment.

Delivering Exceptional Client Service – Team Development

Creating a culture where teamwork, collaboration and open communication with leadership are valued is vital. Hierarchies can breed fear and resentment. Building teams within a firm and with clients requires transparency which fosters trust, and trust leads to lasting relationships and client loyalty.

> *"People buy from people they like."* – Connie T. Carden

In this industry, your reputation for delivering exceptional client service precedes you. Consultants thrive in environments where they can communicate freely without fear of retribution. Happy consultants depend on a work environment where people feel they can openly communicate, even when there isn't a positive message.

If a team member is open but will likely be met with retribution, they aren't going to share information and will quit. As teams grow and more levels of rank come between leadership and the team, everyone must work harder to dissipate the levels of hierarchy and make sure everyone's voices are heard. Happy consultants provide companies with happy clients, and happy consultants deliver exceptional client service.

> **"Attitude OVER aptitude – the most important team message!"** – Connie T. Carden

A positive attitude and a willingness to collaborate are crucial when hiring and developing consultants. While technical skills are important and can be taught, personal attributes such as grit and interpersonal skills are innate and essential for team cohesion.

Adversity is common in team environments. I experienced it firsthand at IBM in 2011 when another woman who believed she was next in line for my position made my initial months challenging. However, after securing my first business deal, the tension dissipated. For much of my career, I was accommodating, but in 2014 at my current firm, I adopted a new mantra: "If not now, when?" This shift in attitude has been noticed and embraced by many of my female colleagues. When you encounter adversity, you need to address it immediately. Left unanswered, problems will grow beyond control. Act quickly and go forward.

In 1983, I didn't dream that in 2024 I would be leading the teams I have in the last 10 years, teams of 500 to 600 people between two accounts: but here I am. I have appreciated each one of them at Consolidated Edison and Eversource. Their teamwork has brought the success that we have enjoyed. When I think of the growth of my teams over the years, I embrace these attributes: 1) the value that diversity brings to the team, 2) the knowledge of each member's goals and challenges, 3) enjoying the team's regular recognition and rewards, and 4) providing developmental opportunities and, most importantly, the chance to give thanks to each other at the end of every day.

Building a Brand

In the 1980s, personal branding wasn't a consideration. There was no social media, internet or "tagging" to manage. We were focused on securing a job and earning a living. My first car purchased in 1983 came with a 14% interest rate, and my paycheck was a mere $17,000 a year. With rent at $500 a month and daily lunches at McDonald's costing $2.12, there was little room to think about branding.

No one was thinking about building a brand when we were paying the rent. There was no vision board, and our MSA team knew every bar in Atlanta that had free food at Happy Hour. I worked. Hard. As my career progressed, I soon realized that my reputation proceeded me. In the utilities industry, people pay attention to your work. In this small industry, it's hard to escape a bad reputation.

As my career advanced, I realized that my reputation was my brand. With a reputation for honesty and problem solving, I am a champion for my team. I deliver on my commitments, no matter how small. In the utilities industry, your work is noticed, and it's difficult to escape a tarnished reputation.

So, the connection was made for me - my actions speak for who I am. In maintaining my brand, I constantly make myself attend seminars, both internally and externally, specifically around SAP, Oracle and Women in Utilities. I look at LinkedIn profiles and write opinion articles. I like to interview smart women and gain advice on subjects other women are interested in. And I am a member of several boards, allowing me to offer advice, opinions and knowledge that people may not know I have.

My Superpower is problem-solving. I consider myself intuitive and aware of my surroundings, often able to anticipate potential issues. Regrettably, there have been times when I ignored my instincts, but I'm quick to assess situations and avoid conflict.

My Kryptonite is my fear of public speaking and the lingering doubt that I have anything meaningful to say. Each public speaking engagement requires practice and mental preparation. As I author this book, I am working on being transparent and truthful. Imagine the difficulty of remembering untruths during a speech while speaking about this manuscript?

For those building a brand, I advise caution with social media. The digital age is a double-edged sword. I recall a senior manager who was targeted by someone with a grudge. A compromising photo was circulated at her workplace, causing distress and embarrassment. The incident underscores the need for careful brand management in the digital era.

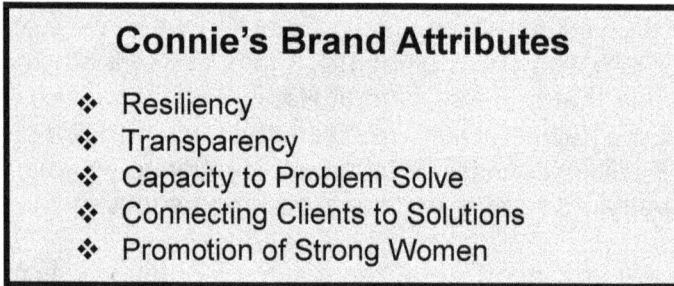

Connie's Brand Attributes

❖ Resiliency
❖ Transparency
❖ Capacity to Problem Solve
❖ Connecting Clients to Solutions
❖ Promotion of Strong Women

Final Thoughts

The most important legacy I have to contribute to the Power and Utilities industry is through the words of this book and by recruitment and retainment of women who love and embrace the industry as much as I have.

I trust that:

1. Women grow, thrive and become senior leadership, and they then recruit and mentor many generations of women for years to come.
2. Women develop a sisterhood which encourages collaboration, and one day statistics will reflect that the percentage of women is greater than men in the client-serving partners who serve this industry.
3. Everyone who reads this book finds their Superpower and finds a job that gives them joy as much as this industry and my clients have given me!

Chapter Highlights	Description
Brand Awareness	Initially not brand aware, started branding building later in career.
Client Relationships	Focus most on client relationships started early in career and has built personal brand on past business success.
Role Model Influence	Her mother, Sarah, who lived a life demonstrating that with determination all things are possible.
Brand Perception Goal	To be perceived as a woman advocate in the utility industry.
Key Achievements	Successful transition from sales to delivery to client champion.
Core Brand Value	Always being transparent.
Client Relationship Strategy	Maintaining visibility and touchpoints with clients, developing professional and personal connections.
Notable Client Experience	Successfully completing major projects with little knowledge of the subject matter.
Professional Development	Member of GridWise Alliance and Women in Power and Utilities within several past firms as chairperson.
Superpower	Problem solving, being intuitive and aware of surroundings.
Kryptonite	Fear of public speaking.
Advice to Others	Be cautious of social media, digital age can be a double-edged sword.

Connie lives in Green Cove Springs and Neptune Beach, FL, with her husband, Clint and her adopted stray cat, Patches. For more information, visit her on LinkedIn at https://www.linkedin.com/in/connie-carden-9823b91/

Chapter 12: Revealing Your Own SuperPower!

Embarking on this venture in the middle of 2023, my initial goal was to draw in, enlighten and keep young women engaged in the utility sector as customer-facing experts. However, as time passed, the mission evolved into something far greater.

The dynamic shifts within the industry, coupled with the technological advancements that bolster it, have broadened my own viewpoint. As I delved into the narratives of these women, it became evident that everyone, not just the women, had their own tales of ascending to prominence within their profession. With the revolution of Artificial Intelligence, everything we learned fifty years ago will be enhanced, and our future utility professionals and the workplace will be even more exciting than before. I am encouraged that these stimulating advancements in an industry that often lags in technology will be enticement to join it.

Each of the nine remarkable women featured here are contributing their distinct experiences and skills to their respective firms, and I am certain that these organizations are honored to have them as representatives. As with Patty Bruffy, even though retired, there are hundreds of women (and men) who can attribute their success to her mentorship over their careers.

Men have also contributed to the narrative of this book, posing questions they've often pondered but hesitated to ask, fearing they might come across as uninformed or overly curious. As the book neared completion, anticipation has built among my stakeholders, clients and friends who are intrigued by the diverse backgrounds represented in this group.

There is one striking distinction I've observed between my male and female colleagues. When posed with the same question, "What is your Superpower?", responses from male colleagues were immediate: "I am a wizard with SAP," or "Distribution is my specialty," and "Clients rely on my guidance for the future." There was no second-guessing. From women, there was always pause. No one answered immediately, regardless of age or work tenure.

This leads to a pivotal reflection for everyone, regardless of gender, as this book concludes: What is my Superpower?

The stories of these women span over five decades with certain aspects changing and others remaining constant. It is through their interviews that they have come to recognize the Superpower they hold and the immense value of sharing that gift with others.

As I've emphasized from the very beginning, if even one individual - woman or man - is inspired to join this industry and finds it as exhilarating and rewarding as we all have, then my endeavors and those of Mary and all nine extraordinary women have been worthwhile.

In closing, we extend our heartfelt gratitude for allowing us to share our journey with you. A special acknowledgment goes out to all the companies that supported the participation of these inspiring women. And thank you to all who made this book happen!

AFTERWORD

Kudos to Connie Turner Carden for penning *Women of Power and Utilities*! Connie is a gifted storyteller, and with each profile readers can really get to know these women, their successes, insecurities and the many obstacles they faced professionally and personally. These women are definitely superheroes in the field of utility software support and services. I personally found insight and inspiration from each profile.

Connie is not only a colleague but a close friend. We are both North Carolina women, raisedz by hard-working, middle-class parents who believed in and encouraged their children to follow their dreams. Connie and I look alike, talk alike and are both driven. We share a love for dancing, Southern food and cheering for our college teams. We both lean into our roots as we share colloquialisms, like 'bless their heart' with authentic Southern accents. In fact, it is not unusual for people to call me Connie and vice versa.

In the work world, Connie is simply a force of nature and is known for getting things done. She is incredibly knowledgeable about technology, really savvy in designing business deals and fiercely passionate about advocating for her clients. Most importantly, Connie supports, nurtures and champions other women who are building their careers in the utility space.

The Book Idea

You might be curious as to how this book came about. Connie and I were in the car together after an industry event when our conversation meandered to the idea of writing. She suggested I write a fourth book which I politely declined. I countered by suggesting that Connie should write a book.

Connie was intrigued and asked how I even got the idea to write my first book and then two more. For me, it is about the personal challenge of doing something out of my comfort zone. Writing a book is not an easy feat. It is a long duration project that at times is filled with frustration. But the reward is immeasurable. An author's copyrighted work is protected by the United States and is a legacy that lives forever. Connie's book, *Women of Power and Utilities,* will ensure that the stories of these women are documented and can be shared with their families and industry professionals for generations to come.

We started brainstorming ideas, and Connie suggested profiling women like herself who are experts and leaders in providing utilities with technology solutions. We had fun considering themes and fell in love with the idea of women as superheroes. Connie continued to build out the concept for the book, shared it with Rod Litke of Innovate UtilityCX (IUCX), who also thought the book idea had great potential and agreed to publish it.

Introducing Clint Carden

Clint Carden, Connie's husband, is not only her biggest fan and advocate, but he also knows hardware, software and services technology across multiple industries. Clint's career began in the US Air Force serving his country for 10 years in many roles, his last being one in technology. After his discharge from the USAF, he achieved great success in Systems Engineering Regional Leadership at Fujitsu (formerly known as Amdahl Corporation) and ended his career as a national services leader for Oracle Corporation in Orlando, serving Oracle's maintenance clients.

Clint met Connie while at Amdahl Corporation. But Clint acknowledged that he had heard about Connie long before he met her. Clint recalls being blown away when meeting Connie in person for the first time. She was simply "drop dead gorgeous," and he found that her reputation for being fearless, fierce and smart were dead on correct.

Connie and Clint started working together on deals, and Clint experienced first-hand Connie's creativity, which Clint notes is Connie's Superpower. Clint recalled their early days working together and quipped, "She would bring me deals, and my response would be, 'Are you crazy?'" She would work the deal in different perspectives that I would have never considered. Clint also acknowledged that in the male-dominated world of technology, credit for the deals came his way, even as Clint worked to direct recognition and accolades to Connie.

Clint recalled that every deal they touched turned to gold. He told the story of a client who wanted their technology suite but with an IBM processor. Clint's immediate reaction was not just "No, but Hell no," as that was the competitor's product. Connie countered, "Why not?", so the agreement was done, the client was ecstatic and the margins on the transaction enviable.

In my interview with Clint, I also got a glimpse of the toll writing this book took not just on Connie but on him. While working on *Women of Power and Utilities*, Connie was also in the midst of delivering a complex SAP customer system for Eversource. Clint recalled that during this process of planning, interviewing, writing, researching, editing and more writing, Connie's free time was minimized. Clint said simply, "The effort and time to write a book is ridiculous." He also lovingly notes, "She has gotten through it, gotten better at writing and became expert at leveraging travel time to edit and review chapter drafts." Clint sees Connie now as more reflective in her current role and passionate about paying it forward and promoting and developing women.

Connie and Clint are a power couple. They love to play together, whether on their boat, jets skis, electric bikes or enjoying dinner at one of the many amazing Jacksonville restaurants. They light up a room when they enter, and their love and respect for each other are clearly evident. They are a delight to be around. Clint proudly notes that his job in life is to promote her. "I support her, plus I love to see her get all the recognition she deserves."

Call To Action

The greatest way we can honor these powerful women is to internalize their wisdom and commit to a personal call to action. As I reflect on which attributes seem to drive the success of these women, there are three important ones that stand out:

Develop Your Brand

Your brand is the unique value proposition you bring to a role or an opportunity. Each of these women honed their personal brands which included skills around establishing trusting relationships, bringing expertise to the challenge, building teams and collaboration, among others.

Take time to consider and build out your own brand. What attributes tell the story of your Superpowers, and which do you deploy to repel your Kryptonite? Are you results-oriented, a change agent, or do you have the ability to build high-performing teams? Perhaps you bring analytical or project management skills. Are you able to take complex topics and share insights in meaningful and understandable ways?

The power of defining your brand is that you can then align your online presence to highlight your Superpowers. Knowing your key strengths will help you evaluate new opportunities. You can ensure your resume and interview reinforce these attributes as you tell stories and present accomplishments that reinforce key elements of your brand.

One of the best ways to really figure out your brand is to write down attributes you believe you bring to your work. Test these key values out with your colleagues, boss, partners and friends. This exercise of getting feedback on your Superpowers will help you refine your brand.

Do What You Love

No job is perfect, and all jobs contain elements that are not my favorites like, for me, doing expense reports. A great role is one that minimizes the less desirable to-dos and offers many opportunities to tap into your Superpowers, while growing new skills. As you consider a new role, ask yourself if this is an organization whose values are meaningful to me? Are there professional growth opportunities at the company? Is this a culture in which I can thrive? Do I like the people with whom I will work?

The adage, 'Do what you love, and you will never work a day in your life,' is true. People who really enjoy and thrive in what they do bring passion to their roles that is naturally inspiring to others. Having a role that you really enjoy helps your mental and emotional wellbeing. Having passion for what you do will unlock your creativity and innovation. The result in doing what you love is enjoying tremendous success!

Support Others

As I reflect on my 35-plus years in the utility industry, there has been a welcome change in women. In my early days, it seemed that some who climbed the ladder made a point to break the rungs so others would not be able to compete with them. I have sadly heard some men comment that 'women eat their own.' But the women profiled in this book demonstrate the power of supporting one another. They added more railings to the rungs and provided instruction so others could ascend even faster.

Challenge yourself to make a resolution to better support others. There are lots of ways to do this, starting with sharing your knowledge and expertise. If you see someone struggling, offer help! Build confidence in colleagues by acknowledging and celebrating their accomplishments. Be a champion for other employees by telling leaders and decision makers about their skills. Consider being a mentor. By supporting each other, we can continue to create success at work and in our personal lives.

Closing

Readers, Connie has shared the stories of nine powerful women who are recognized experts of utility-facing information technology products and business solutions. Their stories remind each of us that the journey is not easy and was never meant to be. Rather, our professional and personal journeys are filled with challenges that require each of us to build upon our knowledge, expertise and collaboration with others to develop solutions that create transformation. As we overcome each and every new obstacle, we can take pride in our success and the development of new technical and emotional skills to position us to take on the next, even more complex opportunities.

Penni McLean Conner

INDEX

A

AAC, 27
Accenture, 30,65,68,69,77,80
Aclara, 78,79,80,82
Amdahl Corporation, 117, 128
Ameren,18
American Management Systems (AMS),90
AMI, 78, 79
Angelou, Maya,21, 25
Appalachian State University, 115
Atkinson, Jeanne, 97
Automation Data Processing (ADP), 28, 31, 32, 35
AVEVA, 54

B

Bailey, Henry, 55, 56
Banks, Kristen, xii
Basrai, Huzaifah, xii
Bates, Debbie, 2,16-26
BearingPoint, 18,65,67,68,117
Bell, Joy, xii
Bell, Lauren Marcellin, xii
Beshkova, Milena, xii
The Blacklist, tv series, 64
BMW Z3,28
Bocelli, Carol and Vincent, xii
Bolen Group, 56,64
Bolen, Jake, 64
Bolen, John, 64
Bolen, Maureen Coveney, 3,52-64
Bose, Chitra, xii
Boston College's Carroll School of Management,79
Brand Attributes:
      Debbie Bates, 24
      Maureen Coveney Bolen, 62
      Patty Bruffy, 13
      Connie Turner Carden, 122
      Lisa Dalesandro DiChristofer, 34
      Michelle Fay, 86

Guthridge, Greg, xii

H
Hanrahan, Kathleen, 21
Hansen, Dean, xii
Harkrader, Kyle, xii
Hawthorne, Bruce, 30
Hayes, Gary,56
Hernandez, Orlando, 101,108,109,111
Hibri, Wael, 19
Hirschey, Mark, xii

I
IBM,19,21,36,39,115,117,120,129
Imlay, John, 115
Innovate UtilityCX (IUCX), xi, 52,128

J
Jackson, Tito, xii
Jacksonville Electric Authority (JEA), 67
Jacksonville, FL, 67
James Madison University, 15
Jefferson, Nellie, 30
Jeffries, Pam, 56
Johnson, Charlie, 68,75,117
Johnson, Mary, x
Johnson, Robyn, xii

K
Kearns, Beth, 4, 89-100
Kennedy, J. Patrick (Pat), 54
KPMG, 65, 117

L
Lawrence, Jared, xii
Leading Quietly by Joseph L. Badaracco Jr., 22
Lehman Brothers, 102
Levine, Ryan, 105i
Lift as I Climb: An Immigrant Girl's Journey Through Corporate America by Jackie Glenn, 22
Litke, Rod, xii, 52,28

Lodestar, 89,90,91
Louis Vuitton, 102
Lynch, Susan, 3, 65-77

M

Management Science America (MSA), 115,116,121
Martin, Brian, xii
McAlary, Julie, xii
McCormack & Dodge, 115
McDonald's, 121
Meredith, Kerri, xii
Meter Data Management (MDM), 89
Miami-Dade Water and Sewer, 67
Microsoft, 68
Minnesota Power, 97
Mississippi Department of Transportation, 66
Morton, Carl, xii
Myers-Briggs, 53

N

NASA, 66
Navigant, 78,80
NCR Solutions, 36,37,39
Neptune Beach, FL, 124
New York University, 17
Newcomb, NicCole, xii
Nexus Energy Software, 79
NiSource, 16,18

O

O'Hara, Cindy, x
O'Keefe, Maggie, 62,64
Oncor, 18
Oracle, 23,25,77,79,89,91,97,101,103,115,117,121,128
Orange and Rockland, 101
OSIsoft, 54,55

P

Page, Rick, 115
Pandemic (COVID Pandemic), 8,101
PBS NewsHour, 103

PI System, 54
Potomac Electric Power Company (PEPCO), 6,7,96
Phelps, Amy, 30
Power Utility Fortnightly, 85,87
PRB Consulting, 7
Price Waterhouse, 79,116,117
Prince Harry, 103
PwC, 65,67,117
Pyles, Sheila and Teben, xii

Q-R
Ravindran, Lakshmi, 2, 36-51
Red Clay Consulting, 89,90,91,92
Richard, Andrea, 64
Riesmeyer, Matthew James, xi
Riggins, Mike, xii
Rogers, Jeffery Lasean, xii
Rogers, Karen, 30
Rutgers State University, 28
Ruzinsky, Ada and Mike, xii

S
Salvucci, Bob, 28
San Onofre Nuclear Generating Station (SONGS), 54,56
Sanders, Kathy, 30
Santa Rosa City Schools, 57,62
Sanzotta, Danielle, xii
SAP, xii, 1, 2, ,3, 27,36,50
Science Applications International Corporation (SAIC), 54
Sciuto, Laura, ix, 4, 101-112
Shah, Mehul, xii
Sharma, Varun, xii
Six Sigma, 53
Smith, Christopher, xii
Smith, Jawon, xi
Soloman, Raquel (Rockie), v,x
Southern California Edison (SCE), 54
Southern Company, 18
SPL Worldgroup, 67
St. Augustine, FL, 35
Stanford, Jamaal, xii

STEM (Science, Technology, Engineering and Mathematics), 1
Superior Water, Light and Power (ALLETE), 97
Surber, Jim, 28

T
TalentQuest, 91
Tarraf, Samia, 69
Thielbar, Bart, 56
Tiffany, 116
Tough, Cathy, 30
Torr, Jordan, x
Trenouth, Ron, xii
Triniti Consulting, 89,90,92,94,97
Turner, James Robert, 113
Turner, Sarah Pruitt, 113

U - V
University of California, Berkeley, 53
University of Central Florida, 65
University of Houston, 90
University of Pennsylvania (Penn), 102
University of San Francisco, 17
Upward Women, 86,88
US Nuclear Regulatory Commission, 54
Utegration, a Cognizant Company, 56
Utterbeck, Hope, 1
Van Reen, Jake, xii

W
Walton, K. Malaika, xii
Wayland, Karen, xii
West Palm Beach Public Utilities, 67,118
What Got You Here Won't Get You There by Marshall Goldsmith, 22
Williams, Albert, 17
Women in Technology (WIT), 21
Wyatt, Mark, xi

X - Y - Z
Yazdi, Mahvash, 55
Year 2000 (Y2K), 7

www.ingramcontent.com/pod-product-compliance
Lightning Source LLC
Chambersburg PA
CBHW050124240326

41458CB00122B/1392